KAYAKING
FOR EVERYONE

FUELED BY
FALCONGUIDES

KNACK

KAYAKING
FOR EVERYONE

Selecting Gear, Learning Strokes, and Planning Trips

Bill and Mary Burnham

Photographs by Stephen Gorman and Eli Burakian

KNACK
MAKE IT EASY

Guilford, Connecticut
An imprint of Globe Pequot Press

Editorial Director: Cynthia Hughes
Editor: Lara Asher
Project Editor: Tracee Williams
Cover Design: Paul Beatrice, Bret Kerr
Interior Design: Paul Beatrice
Layout: Maggie Peterson
Illustrator: Lori Enik
Front Cover Photos by: Stephen Gorman and Eli Burakian; © Ruth Black | Jupiter Images
Back Cover Photo by: Stephen Gorman and Eli Burakian
Interior Photos by: Stephen Gorman and Eli Burakian with the exception of those on page 240.

Library of Congress Cataloging-in-Publication Data
Burnham, Bill.
   Kayaking for everyone : selecting gear, learning strokes, and planning trips / Bill and Mary Burnham ; photographs by Stephen Gorman and Eli Burakian.
      p. cm.
 Includes index.
 ISBN 978-1-59921-509-9
   1. Kayaking. I. Burnham, Mary (Mary K.) II. Gorman, Stephen. III. Burakian, Eli. IV. Title.
 GV783.B87 2010
 797.1'224—dc22

                          2009048394

Printed in China

10 9 8 7 6 5 4 3 2 1

Author acknowledgments

With thanks to our circle of paddling friends who never fail to teach and inspire, with special acknowledgments to Rich Prado and Josh Gregory.

~Bill and Mary Burnham

Photographer acknowledgments

The photographers would like to thank Josie Fisher, Kate Fisher, Rhona Dallison, the Staff at Canoe Imports (South Burlington, VT), Jolyon Rivoir-Pruszinski, and Bud Cherry.

CONTENTS

INTRODUCTION

The journey begins

Call it your personal "aahhh moment," that wonderful feeling that envelops you a few seconds after launching your kayak. The boat glides silently. You take a deep breath and float, soaking in the beauty around you.

Our moment came more than a decade ago. Long before it happened, however, we had to confront a few central questions that you may very well be facing now.

We surmounted our uncertainties and found that a new world awaited us. In kayaks, we've explored salt marshes of Virginia and the Carolinas and tropical mangrove islands in South Florida. We've ridden ocean swells off Maine's coast and weaved through kelp forests passing sea lions and seals off California's coast.

If we could have seen on that first day how this sport would become entwined into every facet of our life, the places it would take us, the friends we would make, and the truly awesome moments we would share as a couple—well, let's just say that for us kayaking, like life, is as much a journey as an activity.

And where will this simple boat and paddle take you? Perhaps on a lake near your home. You may be prepping to run Class I or II rapids or be ready to plunge down the mountain streams pulsing with spring snowmelt or autumn dam releases. You may launch from a sandy beach to paddle with dolphins or head out with a rack of fishing poles for your special spot.

Take a hike—on water!

Kayaking has been described as "hiking on water." Clever and kind of true. Think of the oceans and bays as forests and of the creeks and rivers as trails. You paddle instead of walk, but the effect is the same: You are transported to an amazing world of plants and wildlife that can be reached only by taking the windy tidal creek or running downriver.

We designed this book to take you from the store to the shore and from there out into the water. Our goal is to show you not only how to kayak but also how to do it safely and efficiently. Kayaking—whether a serene day paddle, a weeklong expedition, a short ride with your child, or a few quality hours spent fishing—can unveil a beautiful world. It is a vigorous form of exercise or a form of meditation. It is what you make it.

What you will read here results not only from having done it time and again but also from having often failed first. This is especially true of our whitewater experiences, an area where we still consider ourselves beginners. But, hey, we all have to start somewhere, right?

Where do I start?

Our goal is to make kayaking easy and easy to understand. If you've ever visited a kayak shop, you can relate to the overwhelming feeling that so many choices of boats, paddles, life jackets, and gear inspires.

The first step in understanding is asking yourself a few simple questions: What is it I want to do? Where do I want to go?

This sport has a lot of room for growth. As a beginner, you prefer a stable boat, knowing you won't venture far from land. Perhaps you fish or take photos. Boats with lots of cockpit room are a good choice.

Read this, then seek instruction

At every big change in our skills and commitment to the sport, instruction was the step up we needed.

Mary and I belong to the American Canoe Association (ACA, www.americancanoe.org). This organization offers a range of classes in canoeing and kayaking for both flatwater and whitewater. These classes serve as an excellent introduction to the sport. The British Canoe Union (BCU, www.bcu.org.uk) governs canoe and kayak instruction in the United Kingdom and has a strong U.S. presence as well. This well-respected group offers instruction or "coaching."

A friend and world-class freestyle canoeist, Karen Knight, once shared an insight that has stuck with me for years. After demonstrating her "ballet on water" in a single freestyle canoe, she tossed her paddle onto shore and was handed a shovel. Without skipping a beat, she used the blunt garden tool to accomplish the same moves as she had with her single-blade canoe paddle.

Her point: You can own the best boat, the lightest paddle, the most comfortable life jacket, but the real investment you make in this sport is instruction.

About us

We (Bill and Mary Burnham) are the authors of ten books, including *Florida Keys Paddling Atlas,* a 2008 National Outdoor Book Award (NOBA) winner, and *Knack Car Camping for Everyone.*

We lead kayak trips on Virginia's Eastern Shore half the year. When winter comes, we like to head to the Florida Keys and the Everglades.

Our trips are chronicled on www.BurnhamVirginia.com and www.BurnhamGuides.com. Check out our blogs and post a hello. We would love to hear from you.

RECREATIONAL KAYAKS
They're good for entry-level or beginning kayakers

Call them "pond boats," "poke-around boats," or "surf boats"—by any name, recreational kayaks are fun. They are generally wide, stable, easy to get in and out of, and priced competitively. This makes them popular with beginners, children, older folks, and people for whom paddling is a few hours of serenity on the water.

As with all boats, there are conditions that are tailor-made for recreation kayaks and conditions that are not. Understanding the differences is a ticket to safe and fun paddling.

Their stability makes them useful for anyone who pursues another hobby from the kayak, be it fishing, photography, bird-watching, snorkeling, or diving. Newer materials like thermo-molded plastic make boat weight a nonissue.

A tandem recreational kayak is a good choice for an adult

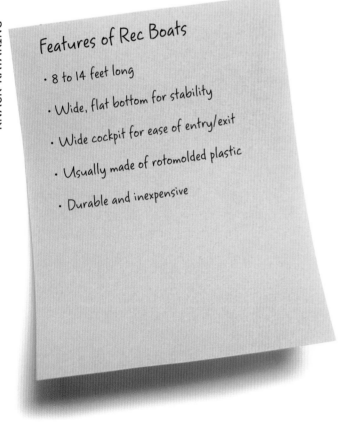

Features of Rec Boats

• 8 to 14 feet long

• Wide, flat bottom for stability

• Wide cockpit for ease of entry/exit

• Usually made of rotomolded plastic

• Durable and inexpensive

Sit-on-top

Look for at least one hatch for items that cannot get wet.

• They are stable, self-draining, and easy to get in and out of, even unassisted from the water.

• They are a good choice for swimming, surfing, fishing, snorkeling, or SCUBA diving.

• You will get wet, so they are unsuitable for cold weather or long distances.

• Gear in drybags or diving equipment can be tied down or bungeed into the open compartments on the bow or stern.

and child, two beginners, or two people of differing abilities or staminas.

You do sacrifice performance. A short, wide rec boat won't track as well as a narrow sea kayak. Edging your turns may be compromised by hull shape and width. Without a skirt, large cockpit rec boats are unsuitable for seas and rough water conditions where there is a risk of taking on water.

It all adds up to is this: Recreational kayaks are great for near-shore paddling, for paddling together, and for short trips in the right weather conditions.

Recreational Kayak

- They are great for paddling on small lakes, rivers, or creeks or playing in the ocean surf near to shore.

- Some models have sea kayak-like features, such as one or two bulkheads, a cockpit with which you can wear a spray skirt, deck lines, and watertight hatches.

- Don't plan on going very far from shore or on an extended touring trip. For that, you need a sea kayak.

Tandem Kayak

- Recreational tandems feature a wide-open cockpit, almost like a canoe. They are stable with lots of room for gear, a third person, or a dog.

- Tandem sea kayaks feature individual cockpits and a more streamlined hull.

- Tandems make it possible for people of differing abilities to paddle together.

- Consider the additional length and weight, likely one hundred pounds, in transporting a tandem.

SEA KAYAKS
These are performance boats for advanced paddling

Properly chosen for your size and ability, a sea kayak can take you places you only dreamed of: sheltered mangrove creeks or rugged ocean coastlines, long open-water excursions or hard-to-reach island campsites.

There are many varieties, yet all sea kayaks share must-have features that make them seaworthy.

They are longer and slimmer than recreational kayaks. A sea kayak has sealed bulkheads fore and aft and a cockpit coaming for attaching a spray skirt. This last feature is essential for performing certain rescues and rolls.

With more refined equipment comes a demand for additional skills. If you wear a spray skirt, you should know how to do a wet exit so you don't panic getting out of the boat.

Many people get into a sea kayak and comment on how

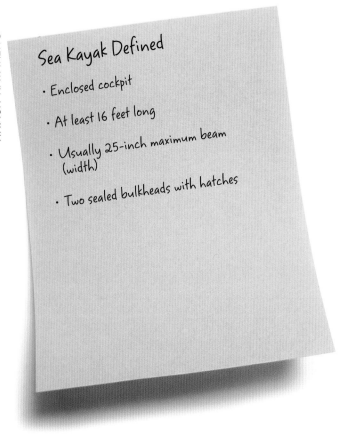

Sea Kayak Defined

- Enclosed cockpit

- At least 16 feet long

- Usually 25-inch maximum beam (width)

- Two sealed bulkheads with hatches

Bulkheads

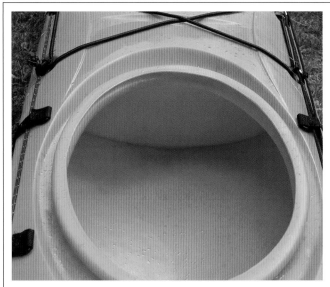

- Forward and aft bulkheads are sealed walls located on either side of the cockpit.

- They form dry storage compartments, called hatches, in the bow and stern.

- They confine water to the cockpit in the event of a capsize, making the boat easier to empty.

- Air in the bow and stern compartments will keep your kayak afloat even when turned over.

tippy it feels. This is a result of the narrow width and hull shape. But this is also an advantage as you learn to hold an edge in a kayak and brace yourself if you're starting to tip.

The unwavering performance formula in the sea kayak world is this: A wider boat is stable and slower; a narrow boat is faster but tippy. It's a trade-off between your comfort zone and desire for performance.

Some people will grow out of their recreational kayak as their skill set advances. In a sea kayak, they will find more room to grow as a paddler.

ZOOM

Get a boat that "fits" you. Hopefully, you'll plan on spending hours sitting in your boat, so it needs to be comfortable! You want good points of contact with feet, thighs, and hips so the kayak will respond to your body. "Try on" a lot of boats. When you find the right one, it should feel like you are wearing it.

Hatches

Each manufacturer has its own hatch cover style. Experiment with them.

- Bow and stern hatches allow access to the interior of the boat for storage.

- Some sea kayaks feature a small day hatch behind the cockpit to keep essential items accessible.

- Storage hatches are made to be watertight but may not be completely waterproof.

- Keep gear that absolutely should not get wet, like clothes and sleeping bags, in drybags.

Deck Lines

- Sea kayaks have lines (rope) running around the deck perimeter.

- They are a safety feature that you can grab hold of during a rescue.

- Bungee rigging crisscrosses the deck both fore and aft of the cockpit.

- Deck bungees can secure spare paddles, a map case, compass, or water bottle.

WHITEWATER KAYAKS
There are designs for all types of rivers—and paddlers

So you've decided to plunge into river running! Unless you're planning a lazy float down the river, this plunge requires a boat designed for fast-moving whitewater conditions.

It was once a fairly simple decision: a short boat that put an emphasis on maneuverability. But today there are numerous options, depending on your skill level, river conditions, and what you want to do on the river.

There are creek boats for narrow runs and big drops. There are river runners that favor stability and tracking. There are playboats, with hard edges and flat hulls designed for acrobatic moves. All come in varying lengths, widths, volume, and hull design. Each variable affects performance. And no matter what the literature says, no one boat does it all.

Visit a kayak shop with a wide selection and ask a

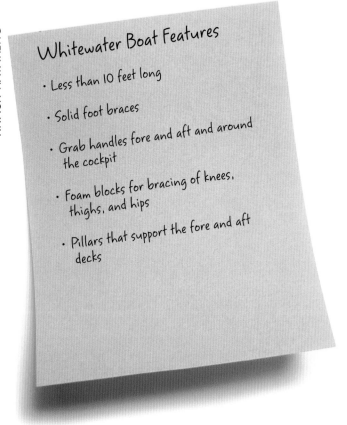

Whitewater Boat Features

- Less than 10 feet long

- Solid foot braces

- Grab handles fore and aft and around the cockpit

- Foam blocks for bracing of knees, thighs, and hips

- Pillars that support the fore and aft decks

Creek Boats

- These boats are generally 8–9 feet long with a rounded hull. The chines are rounded as well, which makes rolling easy but carving turns less so.

- High volume in the bow and stern makes this boat buoyant. It will resurface quickly after submerging.

- A little extra rocker enables creek boats to turn quickly.

- They perform well on narrow creeks with a steep pitch and big waterfalls.

knowledgeable salesperson lots of questions. Talk to other paddlers. Try out as many boats as you can.

Kayak lessons are the ideal way to both demo kayaks and gain the value of an instructor's insight into differences between boats.

If you are not sure what boat is right for you, consider buying a used kayak. This is an economical way to get into the sport. When you fall in love with the thrill of whitewater, you may just end up with several boats in your stable.

River Runners

- The hull is flat, and chines are edgier, allowing these boats to play and surf as they move downstream.

- They have less volume than creekers. This is most apparent in the stern, which is flatter and tapers more sharply.

- Less rocker and longer length enable river runners to track well.

- They are good for big water, including large holes and big waves.

Playboats

- These short, low-volume kayaks are also called "free-style" or "rodeo boats."

- They're designed for surfing waves and holes and doing acrobatic tricks.

- With extremely low volume in the bow and stern and sharp rocker, paddlers can submerge the bow or stern and make the kayak stand on end.

- A flat, or planing, hull makes spinning the boat easy. Hard chines, or edges, on the hull allow the paddler to carve and perform rodeo moves.

KAYAK MATERIALS
Material affects cost, performance, and weight

A variety of materials, whether wood, plastic, or carbon, is used to make kayaks. Commercially, two types are most prevalent: polyethylene, popularly known as "rotomolded plastic," and composites, which have layers of resin and cloth like fiberglass or Kevlar.

The type of material you choose affects price, performance, weight, and durability as well as care and maintenance.

Rotomolded boats handle abuse well, whether bouncing off a submerged river rock or landing on a rough shoreline. White-water kayaks are almost exclusively made of this material.

A recent innovation in kayak material is thermo-molded plastic. It combines some of the rotomolded boat's durability with a rigidity that begins to approach that of composite material.

Composite boat construction represents the high end of

Rotomolded Plastic

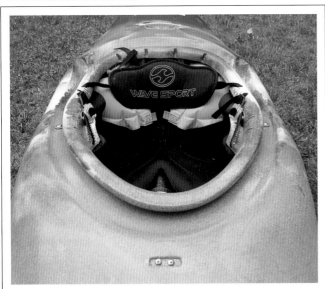

- Plastic boats are inexpensive, readily available, with a diversity of selection.

- Any kayak shop or big-box retailer will carry a selection of plastic boats.

- They have high durability. Within reason, you can drag them across rocks and bang into things without much damage. Even dents can be pulled out.

- However, they are heavy and variations in hull shape are limited by the molding process.

Fiberglass

- Fiberglass boats are light-weight and performance oriented. There is greater variety in design, size, and weight than plastic.

- Fiberglass (and the even lighter Kevlar material) is made by layering cloth and resin.

- A glossy gel coat overlays the fiberglass, giving it a sleek, colorful finish.

- They are expensive. The gel coat surface fades and is prone to cracks, dings, and gouges. Repairs are more technical.

the spectrum. The payoff comes in quality. More precise hull designs translate into higher performance. They are light and they are rigid. In the water, this translates into a more efficient boat.

The big question is this: How will you use your boat? If you drag your boat along shore or paddle in a river or in an area where rocks or oyster beds are common, you may want a plastic boat's durability. If performance is top priority, explore thermo-formed or composite boat options. If you plan on flying to exotic locales, consider a foldable or inflatable boat.

Wood

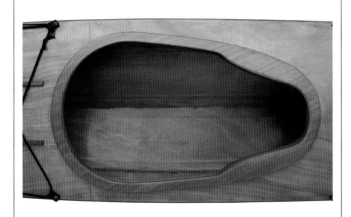

- Lovers of wooden boats will undoubtedly be aficionados of the wooden kayak.

- You can purchase a do-it-yourself kit or have one handcrafted and custom-made for you.

- Wooden kayaks do require more TLC than most other boats (which, if you're an avid woodworker, is hardly a burden).

- Use care when loading for long trips. Too much weight in the hatches of a wooden boat can damage it.

Other Materials

- Inflatable: heavy-duty coated nylon, vinyl (PVC), or rubber.

- Folding kayaks: wood or aluminum frame with a canvas or plastic cover.

- Kevlar: an expensive but lighter substitute for fiberglass cloth (with the added benefit of being bulletproof).

- Carbon fiber: superstrong and ultra-lightweight. Common in high-end paddles and boats.

HULL SHAPE
Characteristics of a boat's bottom greatly affect performance

Hulls can be round, angled, or flat, and each shape affects how the boat handles in the water. All-in-all, hull dynamics are a near-science about which the average kayaker needs to know only a couple of principles: types of hull designs and how they react in water.

As a beginner kayaker, you should experiment with many different kinds of boats and learn how different hull shapes respond to both your skills and body.

As usual, choosing a hull shape involves a trade-off. A feature that gives you maneuverability may not paddle in a straight line. Boat makers continually tweak hull design in hopes of achieving a balance among performance, tracking, and stability.

A perfectly rounded bottom with very little chine stream-

Round Hull

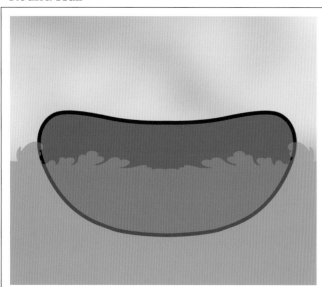

- Rounded, "displacement" hulls are a traditional sea kayak bottom shape.

- Their streamlined shape plows through water efficiently, making them good for touring or river running.

- The bottom of the curve may come to a shallow V,

creating a center line or keel that results in better tracking.

- A rounded hull does reduce maneuverability, but this can be overcome by the paddler's skill at edging and turning.

Chine

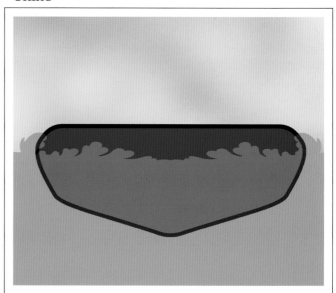

- Chine is the angle formed where the boat's bottom and sides join.

- An abrupt angle is known as a "hard chine." Although initially unstable, this boat can be edged with great stability.

- Medium-chine hulls combine edging prowess with improved stability.

- Boats with soft-chine hulls offer less edging and carving ability but are more predictable and stable.

lines through the water. However, it is almost impossible to edge, decreasing turning ability.

A completely flat bottom is so stable you could probably stand in the boat. But this style performs poorly in even moderately rough water.

Try out lots of boats. Go to an outfitter's demo day or a paddling festival. Ask friends if you can take theirs for a quick spin. You'll likely know within a few minutes if that boat is right for you.

ZOOM

Rocker is the curve of the boat's bottom from bow to stern. Continuous rocker is when the curve is consistent from end to end. Kick rocker is where the ends angle up dramatically, making whitewater play moves easier.

U-shaped

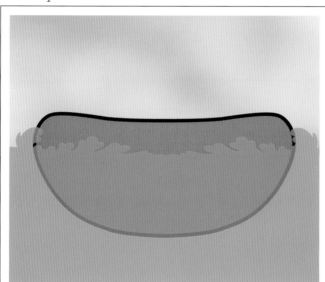

- U-shaped or planing hulls have dramatically flat bottoms and hard chines.

- Whitewater playboats are the extreme example of this type.

- When speed is acquired, the flat bottom literally planes across the water, allowing the boat to do spins, carves, and rodeo moves.

- Flatwater kayaks with a planing hull, although stable, perform poorly in rough water. They also don't track well.

How Stable Is Your Boat?

- If a boat feels stable while at rest in the water, it has good primary stability.

- Test it: With paddle stowed beneath one arm, take a sip from your water bottle. If the boat feels stable, it has good primary stability.

- Secondary stability describes how a kayak feels when it is tilted to one side.

- Test it: Edge your kayak. Does it rest easy on its side? Or is it ready to capsize?

- A kayak with good secondary stability rests easy when edged.

SPECIAL KAYAKS
There's a kayak made for every person and every situation

There are dozens of specialty kayak manufacturers, each with a dozen or more models varying in function and performance.

Say you yearn to travel to foreign locales where quality rental boats may not be available. You could use a folding kayak. Such a kayak packs up into a luggage-sized backpack or duffel bag that can be checked through at the airport.

Inflatable kayaks are another way to go for transportability. However, be sure to get one that is fully seaworthy, not a glorified pool toy. The fabric needs to be extremely tough, especially if you plan on doing whitewater or bumping off rocks.

For those who want to literally jump right into kayaking, the canoe/kayak hybrid is a good option to try. These stable, open-cockpit boats are popular with kayak fishermen as well.

Folding Kayak

- This kayak is comprised of a wood or aluminum tube frame covered with canvas or nylon skin.

- Look for internal chambers called "sponsons" that inflate to tighten the skin and add flotation.

- Options include rudders, storage hatches, integrated spray skirts, and other seaworthy features.

- If you plan on multiday expeditions, be sure to consider the boat's payload capacity: person plus gear and water.

Inflatable

- With a pump, these boats inflate quickly and have you on the water in a matter of minutes.

- They tend to be less expensive and lighter than standard kayaks.

- There are models suitable for whitewater, rivers, surf, and open water.

- Be sure to get one made from tough, high-pressure fabric that has a multilayer floor.

Speaking of fish, kayak fishing has skyrocketed in popularity in recent years. No longer do you need to search for a kayak that fits your needs; manufacturers are making models specifically designed for fishing. Any plastic sit-on-top can get you into the sport of kayak fishing, but if you want to get a little more serious, there are features, ranging from hull design to special accessories, to consider.

Sectional hard-shell kayaks are another option, though not as packable. Such a boat comes apart in three pieces, each with its own bulkheads, and bolts together.

ZOOM

Surf skis are long, narrow (usually less than 20 inches wide), sit-on-top kayaks built for speed rather than touring. They track well but are less maneuverable, so many come with a foot pedal-operated rudder. They are extremely tippy, so lots of practice is required. Fitness kayaks are stripped-down, lightweight craft for those whose main goal is exercise.

Canoe/Kayak Hybrid

- Boats with an open cockpit from bow to stern can accommodate two or three people, gear, and perhaps a dog.

- They vary hugely in hull shape, seaworthiness, and features.

- Some have buckle-in seats that can be moved forward or backward for flexibility.

- These are popular with those who are accustomed to canoeing. You can even use a single-blade canoe paddle instead of a kayak paddle.

Fishing Kayak

Rod holders and live wells are being incorporated into kayak design.

- Fishing requires patience, so you'll want a kayak with a comfortable seat.

- Chasing a shadow or angling the big one will require maneuverability.

- Stability is also important. Some fishing kayaks are so stable you can stand up and cast.

- Some kayaks feature foot-operated pedals for hands-free traveling.

ANATOMY OF A SEA KAYAK
Sea kayaks' features set them apart

True sea kayaks are designed for long distances, multiday trips, rough sea conditions, and advanced maneuvers and rescues.

Sea kayaks are generally longer and narrower than recreational kayaks. They have two bulkheads, fore and aft, and at least two hatches. The cockpit area is enclosed, and the cockpit coaming allows for attaching a spray skirt. Inside the cockpit, thigh braces and adjustable foot pegs or braces help aid both stability and maneuverability.

Because they're longer, sea kayaks are usually heavier than other boats. You can counter this weight by choosing a boat constructed from lightweight material like fiberglass or a carbon-Kevlar mix.

For us, sea kayaks have become our primary vehicle for exploration. We stuff our hatches full of camping gear and

Deck View

- Whether you're in a kayak or a battleship, the front of the boat is the bow, the back is the stern.

- On the bow deck are a carrying handle, perimeter safety lines, deck rigging, recessed compass (optional), bow hatch, and hatch cover.

- Cockpits come in various shapes and designs. Each style affects how easily you can enter or exit the boat.

- On the rear deck are a carrying handle, perimeter safety lines, deck rigging, a stern hatch, hatch cover, and day hatch (optional). A rudder is also optional.

Cockpit View

An adjustable seat backband lets you choose a comfortable setting.

- The flanged edge of a cockpit is called the "coaming." The ridge is for attaching the spray skirt.

- The shape and height (inside height from hull to deck) affect how a boat fits your body. A tall cockpit allows for more leg movement. Keyhole cockpits are snug but

- allow more boat control.

- You can make a cockpit fit better by padding out the thigh braces and seat.

- Foot pegs should be adjustable to your leg length. In kayaks with rudders, foot pegs double as rudder controls.

food, then set off to explore coastlines for up to ten days. We're confident that in a boat designed to track well, we can focus our strokes on moving forward as we make long open-water crossings.

Sea kayaks have also accommodated our personal growth in terms of paddling skills. At first we were challenged because of how unstable they felt. Now we're dancing on the water with deep edges and sweeping turns. As a result, we have confidence in the boats whether having a calm day paddle or battling rough seas.

ZOOM

Comfort: Touring may call for sitting in your boat for hours on end, so comfort is a big factor. Each manufacturer has different mechanisms for adjusting foot pegs, seats, and seat backs. Try them out to see which you prefer. If you are very tall or very short, be sure the foot pegs move forward or back far enough and with ease.

Side View

Bulkheads are located fore and aft of the cockpit.

- Rocker, the curve of the boat's bottom from bow to stern, is easiest viewed from the side.

- Freeboard is the amount of boat that sits above the water. A low freeboard minimizes the amount of kayak exposed to beam winds.

- Gunwale is the upper edge of the side of a boat, so named because on ships, guns were traditionally mounted here.

- Most kayaks feature a stern rudder or a drop-down skeg to aid tracking. Greenland-style kayaks are one exception to this rule.

Sea Kayaking Conditions

- Paddling conditions that require a true sea kayak, rather than a recreational boat, include:

- Long, open-water crossings

- Long distances

- Rough seas and swells

- Expeditions (multiday trips)

- Cold weather/water

13

SKEG VERSUS RUDDER
Sea kayaks have directional control options

Rudders and skegs are small finlike tools that help your boat track (go straight), especially in windy, wavy conditions.

So which is better for maintaining your course: a skeg or a rudder? It really depends on whom you ask. In the kayak world, there are skeg people, and there are rudder people. You won't often find someone who likes both, but there are some paddlers who don't use either.

Rudders can also assist in turning a boat, but paddlers who rely on rudders for this task risk becoming lazy. Turning a kayak is a combination of skills and strokes. Don't let a rudder replace good torso rotation, edging, and stroke finesse.

The skeg-versus-rudder debate rages on: Rudderites point out that skeg cables are prone to crimping, rendering them useless until repaired. They say the skeg box occupies

Rudder Assembly

A small clip keeps the blade in place during transit. Be sure to undo it before you get into the boat.

- A rudder is a fin on the exterior stern deck that drops down into the water.

- The rudder fin is controlled with wire cables that run through the boat into the cockpit and attach to your foot pegs.

- In a beam wind, a rudder can help you go straight.

- A rudder can also help you turn in any condition by letting you simply press one or the other foot.

Rudder Control

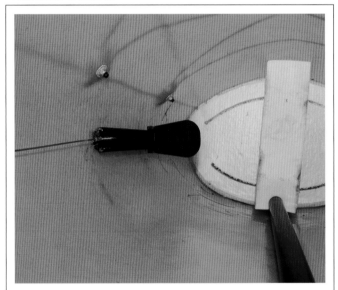

- The rudder fin is dropped down and raised by hand via a rope-and-cleat feature alongside the cockpit coaming.

- The foot pedals inside the cockpit are attached to cables that run to the stern rudder assembly.

- Press the left foot forward, and the boat turns left; press the right foot to go right.

- In a beam wind, you can make slight adjustments to keep the boat straight.

valuable storage space in the rear hatch or that the rudder is better in rough sea conditions.

Skegites argue that rudders create drag and thus sacrifice speed, that they affect the forward power stroke, which requires a solid foot brace, that rudders are heavy and just look plain funny sticking off the end of a kayak.

As you learn more about kayaking, try both, stake your position, and join the great debate.

ZOOM

Installing an aftermarket rudder or skeg: If your boat doesn't come with one, you can purchase an aftermarket assembly. If you're handy, you can probably handle installing a rudder onto a plastic boat. Installing a skeg in a fiberglass or Kevlar boat, however, will require working with fiberglass, perhaps best left to professionals. Either option will probably cost $200 or more.

Skeg Assembly

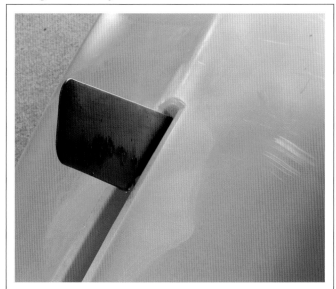

- Sea kayaks are designed to go straight, but in strong winds, all boats will weathercock or lee cock. Weather cocking turns you up into the wind. Lee cocking turns you downwind.

- A drop-down or retractable skeg can effectively alleviate this problem.

- The fin grips the water, straightening the boat and neutralizing the effect of the wind.

- The drag created by a skeg is negligible.

Skeg Control

- It varies by manufacturer, but skegs are usually operated via a sliding lever or a rope within hand reach around the cockpit area.

- The lever controls a cable that drops the fin of the skeg down from a slit in the hull bottom near the stern.

- The amount of skeg that drops down can be fine-tuned using the lever.

- Always remember to retract the skeg before approaching shallow water, or you may damage it.

STORAGE
Hatches provide storage and flotation

In the bow and stern of a sea kayak there are hatches created by sealed bulkheads. The air space provides storage for camping gear, but, more important, it serves as an air pocket. This helps keep a boat afloat when it is capsized or when the cockpit is full of water.

Manufacturers have their own hatch cover styles and means of attachment. Whatever the style, there should be a way for the hatch cover to stay attached to the boat, tethered by cords or straps, to prevent loss during transport.

Access to the fore and rear hatches is difficult when you are seated in the cockpit. Keep that in mind when you're packing your lunch! Pulling alongside a fellow paddler and asking him to retrieve an item is an option. But this should be done only in calm water and never in rough, open seas.

Neoprene Cover

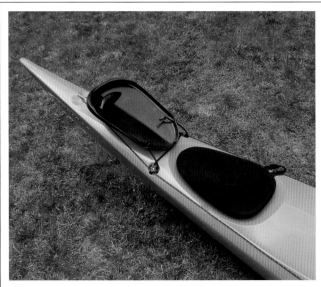

- Many plastic boats have a neoprene cover fitted to the hatch opening. It offers another layer of leak protection.

- The plastic, tethered hatch cover is placed over the neoprene and secured.

- Always be sure to properly attach the neoprene seal, or you risk taking on water.

- Although this method provides a nice, double watertight system, there is always the risk of losing the neoprene or forgetting to attach it.

Buckle Attachments

- A strap and buckle style allows you to ratchet down the hatch cover tightly.

- An adjustable assembly is a good feature for webbing that stretches with age and use or shrinks in the sun.

- The cover is attached via two or three straps, so there is almost no chance of losing the cover.

- Inspect the buckles and webbing periodically because they can wear out with use.

A better option, if it is available on your model kayak, is a smaller day hatch right behind the cockpit where you can store immediate items.

Kayaks without day hatches can be retrofitted with deck bags or under-deck bags where you can stash essential items like a granola bar or first-aid kit.

ZOOM

Hatches can be round, oval, or square, and they come in a variety of sizes. If you plan on taking multiday trips, consider the size of the drybags and other gear you need to stuff into the hatch opening. We've found the large, oval-shaped hatch is the best for large camping gear, from a frying pan to a laptop computer stowed in a special drybag.

Rubber Hatch Covers

Day Hatch

This hatch is located just behind and usually to the right of the cockpit.

Rubber Hatch Covers

- Made of very tough rubber, these snap on firmly like a Tupperware lid.

- This style works with round hatch openings as well as oval hatch openings.

- If they don't come with tethers of cord attached to the boat, be sure to install them.

- Remove this type of hatch cover when storing or transporting your kayak to prevent bulging. Also, apply an anti-UV product, such as 303, to prevent premature aging.

Day Hatch

- A third, smaller hatch is a nice option if it is available.

- By turning slightly (and carefully), you can retrieve objects that you need ready access to while on the water.

- Lunch, first aid, warm clothing items, a radio, cell phone, or other safety items fit easily into a day hatch.

- The day hatch compartment is isolated from the rest of the storage area, so even if it fills with water while open, you will not swamp.

17

ON DECK
Used judiciously, the deck can hold a variety of items

Touring sea kayaks come with deck lines that run around the perimeter of the boat. Attached by recessed deck fitting just above the gunwale line, the cord should be strong and ideally have reflective threads woven in.

If your boat doesn't have deck lines, you can install them. They are often called "grab lines" and for good reason. They offer secure grab points during a rescue, they can be used for

pulling a wet, slippery boat out of the water or for holding on to if you capsize and are treading water while awaiting rescue.

Elastic bungee cords that crisscross the deck, although not suitable for grabbing, are still handy. You can stow a spare paddle beneath bungees on the back deck or slip a map beneath them on the front deck. Bungees directly aft of the cockpit help secure a paddle during reentry.

Deck Lines

- Deck lines are a safety feature that help you grab the boat and hang on in a capsize.

- Items that clip on, like map cases or a compass, can be attached between two deck lines.

- The cord is usually attached to the boat by recessed deck rigging. Inspect it for looseness.

- Deck cord that has reflective threads running through it helps make your boat visible to others.

Foredeck Rigging

- Stretchable bungee cords crisscross on the front deck.

- This is a handy place to slide a waterproof chart case, water bottle, or marine radio.

- Although they stretch over time, bungees can be eas-

ily tightened. When they lose their stretchiness, you should replace them.

- Unless necessary, avoid grabbing bungees or deck lines when lifting your boat. You'll stretch the cords and put stress on the deck rigging.

When it comes to deck storage, our style is minimalism. Our opinion is that too much gear on deck is distracting. It may create wind resistance and reduce aerodynamics, and your boat can even become unstable. If you choose to load up the deck, be sure each item is secured to bungees or deck lines.

ZOOM

Principles of deck storage: Store only those safety and navigation items that you will need. In the event you must store camping gear on deck, be judicious. Items should be either waterproof or in drybags and should be lightweight and compact. Small deck drybags that come with clips to attach to deck lines are available. Use these for necessities only.

KAYAK FEATURES

Rear Deck Rigging

- There should be a bungee configuration to carry a spare paddle.

- Directly behind the seat there are often crisscrossed bungees.

- This is a good place to put your bilge pump or a rolled-up paddle float. Better yet: Wrap the paddle float around the bilge pump.

- This is also a handy place to tuck a small hydration bladder, with the tube running to your mouth.

Items to Keep Handy on Deck

- Spare paddle

- Compass

- Waterproof chart case

- Water bottle or hydration pack

- Bilge pump

- Paddle float

- Marine radio (in a see-through drybag)

19

ANATOMY OF A WHITEWATER KAYAK
Nimble boats designed for fast water

If sea kayaks are like sedans, then whitewater boats are like sports cars. They are meant for windy, fast-moving rivers and are well designed for this environment. They're nimble and easily turned, responsive to paddle strokes and edging moves.

Compared side by side, differences between flatwater and whitewater kayaks are immediately apparent. Whitewater kayaks are shorter. With a few exceptions, they lack hatches,

deck lines, and a rudder (or skeg). But they have other qualities that make them ideal for running rapids, boofing drops, and playing in the hydraulics created by submerged rocks or ledges.

Whitewater boaters outfit their boat for a snug fit. Around the seat, there is extra padding for the hips, lower back, and thighs. Firm, solid foot brakes are a must; boaters cannot risk

Deck View

- The whitewater kayak deck is simple and uncluttered. There are no deck lines or bungees and usually no hatches.

- Handles at the stern and bow give you a place to grab the boat. Some boats feature handles around the cockpit that give swimmers

extra places to grab hold.

- The cockpit is outfitted with a seat and seat back, thigh, knee, and hip braces, and footbrakes.

- You can drain water from the drain plug at the stern end of a kayak.

Pillar

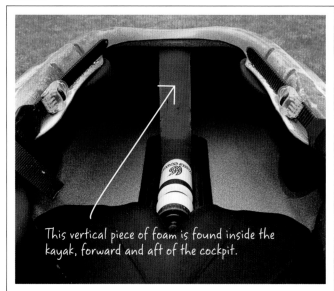

This vertical piece of foam is found inside the kayak, forward and aft of the cockpit.

- The pillar gives structural strength to otherwise flexible plastic kayaks.

- Without a pillar, a kayak may collapse or implode if pinned against a rock by a strong current.

- Some pillars are made of rotomolded plastic and bolted to the boat for extra security.

- Never remove the pillar from your boat. Doing so compromises a boat's structural integrity.

getting their feet stuck or hung up on foot pegs. As a result, foot braces in whitewater boats have evolved from mere foot pegs to more solid designs. Some kayakers fill out the front of the boat with minicell foam.

Structural support is critical for whitewater boats. The power of a rushing river can pin a kayak against a rock and crush it. Pillars inside the kayak help stiffen the body.

On the deck, there may be extra handles that give you more options to grab the boat after the confusion of a dunking.

Thigh and Hip Braces

Snug-fitting thigh and hip braces help you roll, spin, and maneuver.

- A kayak that "fits" your body is easier to control in the water.

- Well-fitted thigh and knee braces help you lock into a kayak.

- Hip pads ensure you won't slip side to side in your seat.

- With your lower body firmly anchored, you can position and paddle with your upper body.

Foot Braces

- A firm foot brace is essential for whitewater kayak maneuvers.

- You can build out a solid foot brace with minicell foam in the kayak bow.

- Many whitewater kayaks today are built with adjustable foot braces.

- Another popular option is an inflatable foot brace that conforms to your foot size and shape. It can be pumped up or deflated while you are seated in the kayak.

WHITEWATER OPTIONS
Here's why whitewater kayakers have more fun

At first glance, the many shapes and sizes of whitewater kayaks can be confusing. Why does that boat have a flat bottom? Why is this boat's bottom rounded? Will hard chines affect how the boat responds in the water? This boat has lots of volume in the bow and stern, but that one has squished ends, like an elephant sat on it. What does it all mean?

Hull design, boat volume and where it is placed around the boat, or boat rocker, and boat width all dictate how the boat will perform on the water.

You can choose a boat with a rounded hull, soft chines, a bit more rocker, and lots of volume in the bow and stern and be a happy creek boater as you navigate steep creeks with big drops.

Or you could go for a flat (planing) hull with bow and stern

Hulls

Hard chines allow for crisper carves and turns.

- Hull style is a big factor in how you use your boat and where you can paddle it.

- The rounded displacement hull of a creek boat gives it stability and buoyancy.

- The flat surface of a planing hull is more typical of river runners and playboats.

- Medium to hard chines are traits of river runners and playboats.

Volume

- Creek boats and river runners may have similar volume, but how it's distributed makes a big difference.

- Volume in creek boats is spread more evenly around the boat, bow to stern.

- Extra volume helps a boat resurface quickly after a big drop. Big blunt ends prevent pinning.

- Low volume at the bow and stern of a playboat—and more volume around the cockpit— gives this boat the ability to dive, making all sorts of trick moves possible.

marked by extreme rocker and low volume. River running wouldn't be ideal in this very twitchy boat, but you could surf all day, do bow stalls and somersaults.

But what if the rivers you run are wide, with huge volumes of water? There are larger holes and big waves, but there also might be more of a distance between these playgrounds. In this case a river runner kayak, with its design tweaks that make it a better tracker, may be the right boat for your conditions.

What it all adds up to is the whitewater kayak is a highly responsive boat that allows quick turns and dynamic moves.

All kayaks are designed for you to have fun. It just seems sometimes that whitewater kayakers have a little bit more!

Rocker

Does your boat "smile"? That means it has a lot of rocker.

- The shape of a boat's hull from bow to stern is called "rocker."

- A boat with high rocker can turn easily.

- The kick rocker of play-boats and freestyle boats is extreme.

- The continuous rocker of a river runner translates into better speed and tracking as you head downriver.

Choosing a Whitewater Kayak

- Demo, demo, demo. Try out as many boats as possible in the conditions you're most likely to paddle in.

- Take a class or borrow a friend's boat.

- Comfort and fit are critical.

- Creek boats are ideal for steep streams and big drops.

- River runners are ideal for low-grade streams and big water.

THE BASICS
Layer clothing for optimum comfort and safety

Whenever you go kayaking, no matter how warm it is or how far you are going, you should always plan for getting wet.

That means you have to plan for not only the air temperature and wind and their fluctuations but also how cold you'll feel wet.

Whether or not you wear a spray skirt will determine what you wear on the bottom. If no spray skirt, you can count on getting wet simply from drips off the paddle. If you do wear a spray skirt, your bottom half will likely stay warmer than your upper half.

Layering is an important principle in any outdoor activity. Several light layers are better than one heavy layer: Take off layers as you get hot and put them back on as the weather changes. However, keep in mind that doing this isn't always

Warm Weather

- Warm-weather paddling requires little more than T-shirt, shorts, or bathing suit.

- Quick-dry nylon shorts or a bathing suit, rather than denim, is best because you will get slightly wet while kayaking.

- Lightweight performance fabrics are great for physical activities because they wick perspiration and dry quickly while providing some warmth and sun protection.

- Footwear should be of the type that can get wet. Water shoes or Crocs are great.

Layering 101

- For cold-weather paddling, start with long underwear of synthetic or wool blend. Never cotton.

- Choose layers made of materials that insulate, allow moisture to escape (known as "wicking"), and will keep you warm even when wet.

- Women can wear bathing suit bottoms rather than cotton underwear.

- Men can wear bathing trunks over their long underwear.

so easy while sitting in a kayak in the water.

When you're on the water, exposed to the elements and the unexpected, clothing is about more than comfort; it's also about safety.

In cold conditions, you want a polypropylene base layer, a fleece midlayer, and a waterproof outer layer. A wetsuit or drysuit are an options addressed on the next page.

YELLOW ● LIGHT

Cotton pulls heat from your body and takes a long time to dry. These traits make it a very poor and potentially dangerous clothing choice in cold environments (hence the phrase "Cotton kills"). Cotton should only be worn in warm-weather paddling, and we don't recommend it in any part of a good layering system.

Layering 102

- A lightweight fleece or wool sweater is a good midlayer.

- A fleece vest insulates the core while allowing ventilation and movement for the arms.

- A wind shirt is made of tightly woven fabric, keeps chill winds out, and is somewhat water-resistant.

- In warmer climates, a lightweight rain jacket will do. It should have a hood you can cinch so it stays on in the wind.

CLOTHING

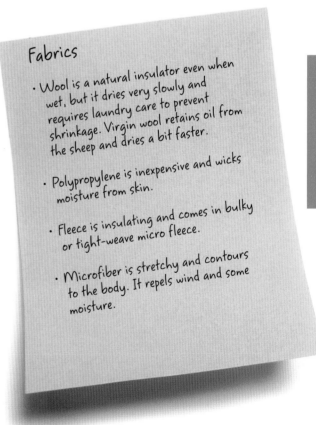

Fabrics

- Wool is a natural insulator even when wet, but it dries very slowly and requires laundry care to prevent shrinkage. Virgin wool retains oil from the sheep and dries a bit faster.

- Polypropylene is inexpensive and wicks moisture from skin.

- Fleece is insulating and comes in bulky or tight-weave micro fleece.

- Microfiber is stretchy and contours to the body. It repels wind and some moisture.

PERFORMANCE FABRICS/CLOTHING
Stay warm in challenging conditions

You have your base layer and perhaps a midlayer; now you need a protective top layer.

There are basically three approaches to cold-weather gear: clothing that is splashproof, wetsuits that keep you warm even if wet, and drysuits that keep you dry even when you are submerged in water.

A spray jacket and pair of paddling pants will protect you from splashes, drips, and waves. This outfit is the minimum you should wear on a cold-weather paddle. Even in warmer conditions, you may want to have these in your hatch in case the weather turns. Remember that you always feel colder when you're wet. Hypothermia can happen even in summer.

An upgrade and the ultimate in performance paddling clothing is the drysuit. Rubber gaskets at the neck, wrists, and ankles

Waterproof Outer Layer

- A waterproof spray top or hooded anorak and a pair of paddling pants are must-have pieces of equipment.

- Rubber or neoprene gaskets at the neck, wrists, and ankles keep out water. It's helpful to have adjustable cuffs for comfort.

- The jacket should be loose-fitting to allow a full range of movement.

- The neck should be zippered to allow ventilation.

Wetsuits

- Neoprene wetsuits keep you warm when you are submerged, even in cold water.

- The neoprene traps a thin layer of water next to your skin, which keeps you warm. They must fit snugly to be effective.

- Thicknesses vary from 1.5 millimeters to 7 millimeters or more, but more than 3 millimeters can impede movement.

- Various styles, from shorties to overall styles called Farmer Johns and Janes, to full bodysuits, expose more or less of the body.

keep water out and keep you dry even when you are submerged. They are superwarm and don't breathe (wick) well, so don't wear too many layers underneath, or you will overheat.

Another way to go is the wetsuit, the kind that divers wear. Made of neoprene, wetsuits are available in varying thicknesses and styles. They keep you warm even when you are completely wet.

Properly fitted clothing is your primary defense against cold. And remember that several loose layers of warm clothing insulate better than one tight layer.

Drysuits

Women's styles often have a drop seat in the back to make urinating easier.

- These heavily designed (and expensive) suits are effective at keeping water out.

- They are made of waterproof fabric, either coated or laminated. Breathable laminates like Gore-Tex help wick perspiration.

- The neck, wrists, and ankles have rubber gaskets that keep water from entering the suit.

- A waterproof zipper should run up the front of the suit. Some suits feature "relief zippers" for answering nature's call.

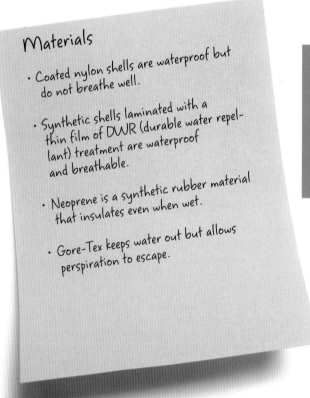

Materials

- Coated nylon shells are waterproof but do not breathe well.

- Synthetic shells laminated with a thin film of DWR (durable water repellant) treatment are waterproof and breathable.

- Neoprene is a synthetic rubber material that insulates even when wet.

- Gore-Tex keeps water out but allows perspiration to escape.

CLOTHING

HEADGEAR
Protect your head from sun, cold, and injury

A sturdy helmet is standard gear for whitewater paddlers. Even on a wide, easy river, there is always the chance of flipping and hitting your head on a rock or limb.

You lose a tremendous amount of body heat from your head. A warm wool or fleece hat is the best way to stay warm on the water and off. A cap can also be covered with a hood to keep rain off.

We've done a lot of paddling in Florida, so sun protection is always a part of our paddle plan. There is no shade on the water, and the sun in southern climes shines much, much stronger than in other areas.

Ball caps and visors protect only your forehead, eyes, and upper cheeks, leaving your neck, ears, and scalp (common places for skin cancer) completely exposed.

Helmet

- Whitewater paddlers should always wear a helmet specifically made for the sport.

- A full-cut helmet has ear flaps and a back that extends down to protect the neck.

- The chin strap should be snug but not uncomfort- able. A good test is to be able to fit two fingers between strap and chin. The helmet should not shift when you wag your head from side to side.

- In cold weather, you can wear a tight neoprene skull cap under the helmet for insulation against heat loss.

Warm Hat

- A warm wool or synthetic fleece hat is one of the easiest and best ways to stay warm.

- Be sure it's made of material that will insulate even when wet (not cotton).

- Caps are small and lightweight, so it's easy to keep one in your day hatch or essentials drybag.

- A close-fitting skull cap will also keep you warm while moving around camp or even while sleeping in the tent.

We prefer wide-brimmed, lightweight, foldable hats of quick-drying material. You can also soak a canvas hat in water to keep you cool while it dries.

You should still wear sunscreen on your face because the sun will reflect off the water and up under your brim.

Hoods and rain hats with visors that can be cinched down keep water from dripping onto your face and spray from getting into your eyes. Neoprene wetsuit hoods are another option for whitewater paddling.

Sun Hat

An adjustable chin strap keeps the hat from blowing off.

- A wide-brimmed hat will not only protect you from the sun but will also keep you cooler.

- Another option is a ball cap with a flap that comes down to cover the neck and ears.

- Look for hats that fold up or can be stuffed for easier stowing at the end of the day.

- Quick-drying or water-resistant fabrics are best for water sports.

Rain Hat

- Waterproof material and a sturdy brim make for the best protection in rain and cold.

- The brim keeps water from dripping into your eyes, while waterproof material such as Gore-Tex keeps your head dry.

- Cinches will help keep it from blowing off and spray from getting in.

- If you don't have a hat, a hood with a visor on your paddling jacket also works well.

HANDS & FEET
Keep these comfortable for hours of enjoyable paddling

Even the most well-coordinated layering system leaves two body parts exposed: your hands and feet.

And as it happens, we can almost guarantee that these two areas will get wet: your feet as you step into and out of your boat and your hands as water drip-drip-drips off the paddle blade.

The temperature of the air and water and the wind chill factor often determine what you wear on your hands and feet. Still, a good pair of gloves and shoes should be considered year-around accessories, not just cold-weather gear.

In warm weather, gloves can help prevent blisters, especially on long trips. In cold weather, a pair of neoprene gloves will keep your hands warm in spite of wetness. If you prefer mitten-style hand gear, check out pogies.

Warm-weather Footwear

Get Crocs with a heel strap to keep them on your feet when you are walking in the water.

- In warm water and air temps, a pair of lightweight Crocs is great because they have treaded soles and holes that let water drain out.

- Water shoes with treads are another good option, as are webbed sandals or hybrid sneaker-sandals for water sports.

- In a pinch, just wear an old pair of sneakers you don't mind getting wet.

- Flip-flops are not recommended because they can fall off in the water. And sandals with straps have the risk of getting caught on a foot peg during a wet exit.

Booties

- Thin neoprene socks can be worn under sandals or Crocs.

- More substantial booties sometimes come with treads, eliminating the need for socks.

- Full-on neoprene boots have flexible, durable soles.

The neoprene uppers feature a zipper for easy on-and-off.

- A reminder: This footwear will keep your feet warm but not dry. Don't be surprised if your feet look pickled at the end of the day!

Footwear can be as casual as a pair of rubber water shoes. In cold climates, footwear can be as heavy duty as a pair of knee-high boots with thick soles.

Depending on where you paddle, shoes might be considered a piece of safety gear. Sturdy soles are invaluable if you launch and land on rocky shorelines or oyster bars. Even in sandy areas, you can't always know what's on the bottom.

Boots will protect your feet from sharp shells and broken glass.

CLOTHING

Rubber Boots

- High boots like British wellies are good for cold weather because they keep your feet dry.

- Some come with felt inner soles. If not, wear an insulating sock underneath them.

- Large boots can add 1 inch or more to your foot clearance inside the boat.

- Be sure to test them out by wearing them while seated in the boat to ensure there is enough room for them.

Gloves

- Choose gloves for what the weather conditions warrant.

- Lightweight paddling gloves with three-quarter-length fingers are good in warm weather for sun and blister protection.

- Full-fingered paddling gloves with articulated (prebent) fingers are better for cold weather.

- Neoprene pogies are mittens that attach to the paddle, favored by white-water boaters because they allow you to feel the paddle shaft.

31

CLOTHING CARE
Take care of your investment

Let's face it: Good gear isn't cheap. You've taken the time to find the right clothing for your paddling conditions. Now it needs proper care to last you a long time.

Leaving a pile of gear wet will shorten its life expectancy and efficacy, especially if you've been in salt water.

Much of the time, all you need to do is hose off or dunk your gear in clean water to remove salt or loose sand or soil.

Washing certain gear in a washing machine will shorten its lifespan. Sometimes all that's necessary is a run through the rinse cycle. Many detergents, especially liquids, can degrade the DWR (durable water repellent) treatment. Use a gentle powdered detergent in smaller quantities than you would use for clothing. Never use fabric softener, dryer sheets, or bleach on performance clothing.

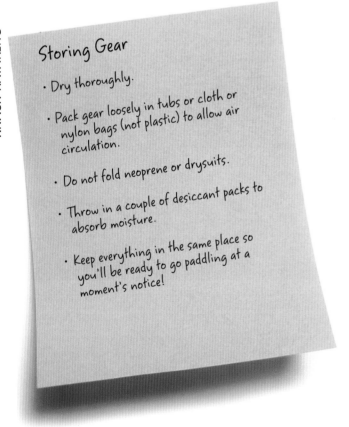

Storing Gear

- Dry thoroughly.

- Pack gear loosely in tubs or cloth or nylon bags (not plastic) to allow air circulation.

- Do not fold neoprene or drysuits.

- Throw in a couple of desiccant packs to absorb moisture.

- Keep everything in the same place so you'll be ready to go paddling at a moment's notice!

Washing

- Always follow the washing instructions on the item's care tag.

- Wash synthetics (polyester, polypropylene, nylon, and so forth) with powdered detergent, not liquid, which can degrade DWR (durable water repellent) treatments.

- Tumble dry on low in the dryer is normally recommended. Do not use fabric softener or dryer sheets.

- Wool is the exception: Always cold wash on delicate cycle. Air dry on a flat surface, not in the dryer.

Clean and dry your gear as soon as possible after getting home. If you wait until you are packing for your next trip, you may find that items have succumbed to mildew or even damage.

Check for any damage to zippers or fabric, dry thoroughly, and store in a cool, dry place.

Neoprene

- Neoprene can get stiff and shrink with age if not properly cared for.

- Much of the time simply rinse with fresh water. If the item is heavily soiled or begins to smell slightly mildewy, hand wash with special neoprene wash.

- Allow to dry completely but not in the dryer or in direct sunlight.

- Do not store neoprene folded. Doing so creates creases.

Waterproof Clothing

Drysuit gaskets require special attention.

- Putting them into the dryer on low for thirty minutes can restore DWR coating.

- When necessary, use a nonaerosol spray to restore DWR finish to soft-shell garments like paddling jackets, pants, and drysuits.

- Wash-in waterproofing that works in the machine is also effective.

- Apply 303 Aerospace Protectant to drysuit gaskets and allow to completely dry. Dust gaskets with baby powder and store.

CLOTHING

33

PERSONAL GEAR
These items are essential for comfort and safety

Your small bag of personal gear can be as essential as a piece of clothing. We carry a small, personal drybag in the boat at all times, either in a day hatch or in the cockpit. It's there for quick access for a variety of comfort or safety gear.

The type and amount of personal gear you bring will vary, depending on how far and how long you plan to be out, the weather conditions, how far from civilization you'll be, and who is going with you (that is, children or inexperienced paddlers).

When we guide trips, we usually bring more items to assist others. When it's just the two of us out for a day paddle, we can take less, but there are certain items we always have. These include a headlamp, toilet paper, cell phone, first aid kit, and sun protection.

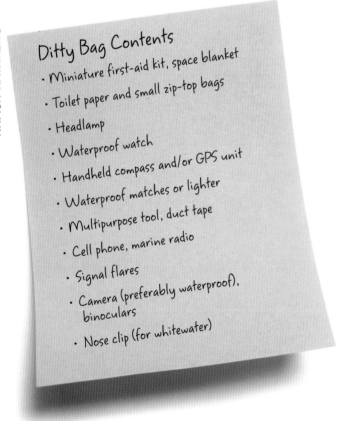

Ditty Bag Contents
- Miniature first-aid kit, space blanket
- Toilet paper and small zip-top bags
- Headlamp
- Waterproof watch
- Handheld compass and/or GPS unit
- Waterproof matches or lighter
- Multipurpose tool, duct tape
- Cell phone, marine radio
- Signal flares
- Camera (preferably waterproof), binoculars
- Nose clip (for whitewater)

Personal Items

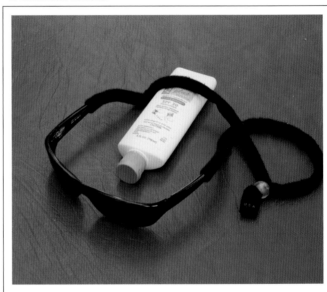

- Protection from the sun is important, especially in southern climes. Bring sunscreen and lip balm with appropriate SPF.

- Sunglasses you want to keep should have floatable Croakies to keep them on your head and retrievable if they fall off.

- A small spray bottle of insect repellant is good to have.

- Don't forget toilet paper or tissue for necessity stops and small zip-top bags to pack it out.

After trial-and-error and more time spent on the water, you'll pare down and add to your necessity bag to suit your needs. Each paddler should be responsible for his or her own personal gear.

Periodically check the expiration dates on items like flares and first aid items and the charge left in your spare batteries. Replenish as needed.

······· GREEN ● LIGHT ·······

Protecting electronics: Consider clear, voice-through drybags for your cell phone and GPS unit. The soft plastic allows you to push buttons and talk through without exposing the electronics to the elements. Be sure to tether it to your life jacket or a deck bungee in case you drop it.

Tools

- Always have a headlamp or small flashlight in case fog or darkness falls before you get in.

- Don't forget extra batteries.

- A Swiss army knife or multi-purpose tool will come in handy for a variety of uses.

- Pack binoculars for bird-watching and spotting far-off nautical markers.

Water and Energy Snacks

- Adults may require up to three or four liters of water for a full day of strenuous paddling—more if the weather is hot and humid.

- For overnight trips that require cooking, the general rule is one gallon per person per day.

- Have some easy-grab snacks in your ditty bag for quick energy.

- Granola, energy bars, beef jerky, dried fruit, or packable fresh fruit like apples make for easy quick-grab snacks.

TYPES OF PADDLES
The decision and the expense are second only to the kayak itself

The types of paddling you do—whitewater, touring, recreational, or surfing—will call for different styles of paddle. Blades come short and wide, or long and narrow. Shafts can be shorter or longer. Materials range from plastic to fiberglass to wood to carbon fiber—or a combination.

It pays to pay attention to these choices. You will rely on this piece of equipment not only for moving you forward for hours on end but also for elegant turning, sculling, and perhaps rolling. Most experienced kayakers have a favorite brand and style they have fallen in love with.

A beginner paddler risks putting all their money into the boat, then skimping on a cheap paddle. With rare exception, price is conversely proportional to weight: the lighter the paddle, the higher the price. We believe that your level of

Recreational Paddle

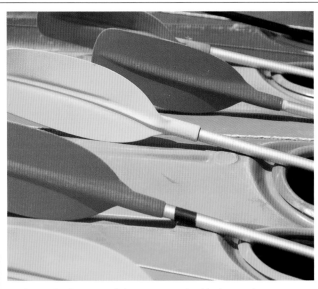

- This is the bottom of the line or the type likely to come with a rental.

- Such paddles usually feature a plastic blade and an aluminum shaft.

- The blade may be rectangular, without much flare, with a straight power face and rib on the back.

- They are inexpensive but quite heavy. They are an OK choice for your spare paddle.

Euro Paddle

A button in the middle of the shaft allows you to feather the blade or break the paddle apart entirely.

- The Euro-style paddle is so-called because it comes from European-inspired designs.

- The blade is asymmetrical, with the top edge longer than the bottom edge.

- The shaft should come apart in the middle for ease of transport and be adjustable for feathered or unfeathered paddling.

- It can be made of plastic, fiberglass, carbon fiber, or a combination.

enjoyment on the water directly corresponds with the lightness of your paddle.

It's pretty simple: Consider how many times in an hour you will lift your arm to plant the blade in the water. After several hours, even a few ounces will make a huge difference in how heavy a paddle feels—and how long you feel comfortable staying out on the water.

In terms of money and effort, you will pay for every ounce, or lack thereof. The best and lightest paddles are made of carbon fiber and can cost $300 to $400. For those who paddle for a living or who like to rack up 15 to 20 miles in a day, it's an expense gladly paid.

For day paddlers, a combination of materials, such as a carbon shaft and plastic blades, is a good compromise that could save you $100 or more.

If you truly intend on going out for only a few hours, a plastic recreational paddle will suffice. As long as you understand that your arms will tire out.

Whitewater Paddle

- As with the Euro paddle, the blade is asymmetrical, with the top edge longer than the bottom edge, with a concave face.

- The difference is that the paddle blade and the paddle itself are usually shorter. Also, the shaft is usually one piece, rather than adjustable.

- Materials are plastic, carbon fiber, fiberglass, or a combination.

- Due to the chance of hitting rocks or limbs, the whitewater paddle should be tougher than the lightest carbon fiber touring paddle.

Greenland Paddle

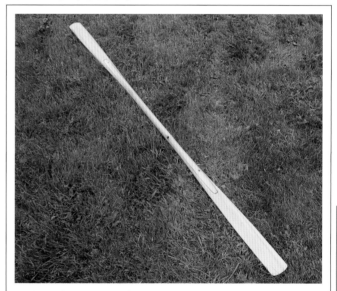

- These descendants of the ancient Greenland-style paddle are popular with some sea kayakers.

- They are almost always one-piece, unfeathered, and made of wood.

- They have narrow, symmetrical blades and are usually longer than Euro paddles.

- Their use requires special finesse, so practice is required. Keep a Euro paddle as your spare until you are proficient.

PADDLE FEATURES
Try out many styles to determine the best one for you

Just as your boat should fit you and have the right features and accessories, so should your paddle. You should try out as many styles and sizes as you can in order to find the one that fits right.

The material that a paddle is made of is the major factor affecting weight, performance, and price. Generally speaking, plastic is at the heaviest and cheapest, while carbon fiber is the lightest and most expensive.

Paddle length is measured in centimeters and typically ranges from 210 to 240 centimeters. The best length for you depends on your body size, the beam (width) of your boat, and your paddling style.

Women, children, or anyone with small hands may want to consider a paddle shaft that is smaller in diameter and thus

Anatomy of a Paddle

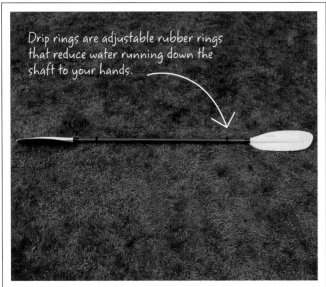

Drip rings are adjustable rubber rings that reduce water running down the shaft to your hands.

- A kayak paddle is two blades at either end of a round shaft.

- Where the blade tapers to the shaft is called the "throat."

- This efficient design means you always have a blade ready to plunge into the water for power.

- The shaft can be straight or bent at the hands, one piece or two piece.

Blade Design

The blade's top edge is longer than the bottom edge.

- There is a variety of blade designs.

- The blade of this sea kayak Euro-style paddle is long and asymmetrical.

- The blade's power face is smooth and concave or scooped.

- The rib of the paddle shaft is evident on the back face of the blade.

more comfortable to grip over extended periods of time.

An ergonomically-inspired bent shaft puts your wrists in a more comfortable position, thus reducing stress and fatigue on the joints.

Finally, you can choose between a one-piece or two-piece paddle. The latter is recommended for portability as well as the ability to feather or unfeather the blade. Whitewater paddlers may prefer a one-piece shaft for its rigidity.

Blade Size

- Blades may be short and blunt or long and narrow.

- A blade with a larger surface area gives you a greater bite in the water for quicker acceleration.

- However, a larger blade adds weight and may add to fatigue on a long day of paddling. Smaller blades offer less wind resistance.

- Dramatically spooned blades can add to your speed but do require some finesse to use.

Feathering

- Blades can be feathered to offset at an angle of between 60 and 90 degrees.

- With an unfeathered paddle, both blades are in the same plane.

- A paddle should be adjustable via simple buttons or a gear in the middle of the shaft.

- Experiment with both styles—feathered and unfeathered—to learn which set up you prefer.

ACCESSORIES

LIFE JACKETS

A proper-fitting personal flotation device (PFD) is a vital piece of equipment

Also known as a "personal flotation device" (PFD), the life jacket is more than an accessory or afterthought. We firmly believe that every paddler should wear a properly fitted, Coast Guard-approved jacket at all times. And it should be zippered and buckled, not flopping around loose.

The U.S. Coast Guard requires everyone on any recreational boat have an approved flotation device on board and within easy reach.

If you do choose not to wear it, it must be accessible, stowed behind your seat or under your deck bungees. Do not put it into your hatch, where it will do you absolutely no good in an emergency.

Touring PFD

There should be several compression straps for fine-tuning the fit.

- Consider a low-profile vest that concentrates the floatation around the waist.

- Low-profile PFDs offer good range of motion with your upper body and arms for various strokes and maneuvers.

- Pick a vest with bright color and reflective tape for visibility.

- If it doesn't come with one, you should attach an emergency whistle to the shoulder strap.

Women's Fit PFD

- Today most manufacturers make PFDs specifically designed with the female frame in mind.

- These PFDs have scoop-outs in the foam to accommodate larger breasts comfortably.

- The cut in the back should be higher to keep the PFD from hitting the kayak seatback.

- Experiment with snap buckles and front and diagonal zippers to see which is more comfortable and easy to use.

If you're in a situation where you need it—rough seas, a collision with a powerboat, an injury, or a capsize—you're not going to be in very good shape to get to the PFD and put it on. Try doing that while treading water and holding on to your boat and your paddle.

Finding the right PFD for your body size and shape is simply a matter of trying on as many as possible. Experiment with vests that zipper in the front and then try on one that zips on the side. If you want handy access to things like bug spray or sunscreen, consider a PFD with a front pocket.

Children's PFD

- Be sure your child's PFD is Coast Guard approved, not a pool toy.

- It should be of the proper size for the child's weight.

- It should have a grab loop at the back of the neck for retrieving the child from the water.

- Kids must wear PFDs at all times on the water, no exceptions.

Whitewater PFD

- Choose a vest with minimal accessories on the front. Pockets, loops, and tabs are all a risk for snagging.

- Think streamlined. A side-zipped jacket keeps the front of the vest clean.

- A small piece of square black plastic called a "knife tab" is a handy spot to store a rescue knife.

- A low-profile vest protects the chest and torso while allowing for good range of motion for strokes.

ACCESSORIES

SPRAY SKIRTS
Wear a skirt to keep water out of your cockpit

Spray skirts aren't just for whitewater or expert paddlers. Once you start paddling more often, you'll find a spray skirt to be an essential piece of gear to keep splashes and annoying drips out of your cockpit. Wearing one can keep your legs from getting sunburned. In cold weather or rough seas, a spray skirt is a safety device as well.

The biggest fear of most beginning kayakers is that their boat will flip and that they will somehow get stuck in the cockpit upside down, trapped by the spray skirt. We have to admit that it was on our minds the first time we tried one. Now we feel naked without one!

Although this is a remote possibility if the skirt is too tight around the coaming, in reality your body weight will pop you out of the cockpit, and your life jacket will buoy your head to

Nylon Spray Skirt

A cross-rib arches the skirt to keep water from pooling.

- Skirts made of nylon are lightweight and easy to put on and take off.

- While not as effective as a neoprene skirt in keeping water out of the cockpit, they are suitable for day trips in calm weather.

- A nylon spray skirt is cooler in hot weather and usually more adjustable than full neoprene skirts.

- They may have special features like suspenders, pockets, cross-ribs, an adjustable tunnel, pockets, and loops with which to attach a map case.

Neoprene

- Neoprene spray skirts are durable, snug-fitting, and effective at keeping water out of your cockpit.

- Whitewater kayakers prefer neoprene spray skirts for this very reason.

- This style costs more, but it is the best kind if you plan on rolling your kayak or paddling in heavy weather.

- If you don't like the feel of putting on a tight girdle, look for an adjustable waist of nylon and Velcro.

the surface in a matter of seconds.

That said, if you wear a spray skirt, you need to know how to do a wet exit (see page 122). Practice in a controlled environment so you do not panic when it happens.

Important: To remove your spray skirt from the boat, pull the grab loop forward toward the bow and then pull up. Simply pulling up won't work.

Putting on a Spray Skirt

- Sit in your boat with your paddle safely stowed underneath a bungee or within reach.

- Reach behind your seat back and tuck the edge of the skirt around the cockpit coaming.

- Move forward slowly and methodically, stretching the skirt around the coaming.

- Be sure the back does not slip off. If it does, you need to start over.

Finish at the Front

Be sure the release strap is outside.

- Keep both hands moving around the cockpit coaming.

- If it keeps slipping off, rest your forearms and elbows along the sides of the coaming to keep it on.

- Complete by slipping the release strap around the front coaming.

- Be certain the release strap is outside, not tucked into the spray skirt. You need to be able to grab it and pull it forward (not up) in a capsize situation.

ACCESSORIES

NAVIGATION AIDS
Always take a nautical chart

So you're going out for only a couple of hours in waters you know like the back of your hand. Who needs a compass or even a map?

But the unexpected can always happen, especially on the water. Inclement weather may come up, or you may decide you want to go a little farther this time, just to see what's around the bend.

For most day paddling, a nautical chart, approved for navigation, will suffice. Get the waterproof kind or stick it into a plastic map case. Slip it under your front deck bungees so you can follow your route at all times.

You should learn to read a chart and use a compass (see Chapter 14), whether it's a handheld or deck-mounted type.

If you're planning a true expedition into wilderness, you

Nautical Charts

- These maps of waterways and shorelines are made with the mariner—both recreational boater and ocean-going vessels—in mind.

- Charts feature special marks and notes that help boats navigate safely.

- Visit your local outfitter or marina and ask about nautical charts of the local area.

Compass

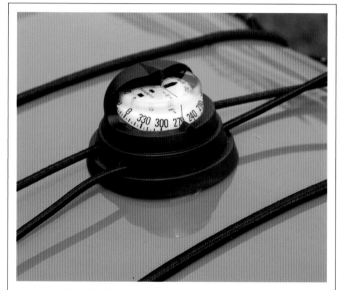

- Using a handheld compass and chart, you can take a bearing on where you'd like to paddle.

- A deck compass enables you to "hold your bearing," or steer your point on a bearing, toward your desired destination.

- Some sea kayaks have a recessed fitting for a deck-mounted compass.

- A less expensive alternative is a deck compass that attaches with clips to your deck lines.

will want to have a variety of navigation tools at your disposal, like parallel rules and dividers to plot a route and measure distance.

Handheld GPS (Global Positioning System) units are terrific aids to navigation. Basic units start at less than $100 but may not have all the features you want, such as mapping capability.

Handheld GPS Unit

Even if it is "waterproof," protect your unit in a special drybag.

- A Global Positioning System receives information from satellites orbiting the Earth and gives you the coordinates for your position.

- Coordinates are given in longitude and latitude, such as N25 08.700 W80 23.842.

- When you punch in the coordinates of a desired destination, the unit will point in the direction you should go.

- Read the instructions that came with your GPS unit and practice using it. Always carry extra batteries when you paddle.

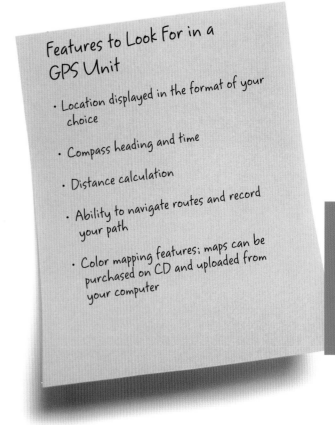

Features to Look For in a GPS Unit

- Location displayed in the format of your choice

- Compass heading and time

- Distance calculation

- Ability to navigate routes and record your path

- Color mapping features; maps can be purchased on CD and uploaded from your computer

ACCESSORIES

WATERPROOF STORAGE
Keep your gear dry for safety and comfort

Even though kayak hatches are designed to be watertight, they often leak slightly, especially if rough seas wash over your boat. Anything you absolutely don't want to get wet should go into a drybag or drybox. There are so many varieties of dry storage on the market that you could probably find a different one made for each and every piece of gear you have, from sleeping bags to small electronics.

The great benefit to drybags is that they can be folded down to compress around items snugly and stuffed into a hatch opening.

Clear drybags made for electronics enable you to keep them accessible yet protected from splashes, drips, and dropping. For example, we always keep a handheld marine radio in a soft, voice-through drybag tucked under our front

Drybags

Drybox

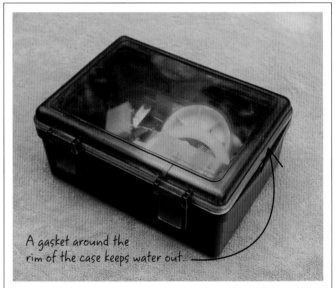

A gasket around the rim of the case keeps water out.

- Drybags come in many colors and sizes, and are usually numbered or sized according to their capacity.

- For example, SealLine's Baja 5 drybag has a five liter capacity. NRS's extra-small Tuff Sack drybag holds six liters.

- Bags with compression straps make large stuffables, like sleeping bags or a tent, smaller and easier to fit in a kayak hatch.

- Clear bags shaped to fit a GPS unit, cell phone, or marine radio are soft so you can operate and talk through the plastic.

- Hard-sided waterproof boxes like Pelican brand dry boxes come in a variety of sizes and colors.

- Small, clear boxes are the perfect size for a cell phone and perhaps your car keys.

- Larger boxes can hold and protect expensive camera

or video equipment. The interior is usually foam-lined for shock resistance.

- Keep in mind the size of your hatch openings. If a dry box is too large to fit, you may have to strap it to the deck of your boat.

deck bungees. This way, to respond to an emergency or to hear the weather, we don't have to open any hatches.

Be sure to check your drybags for holes or tears periodically. This can be done by holding each bag up to the light and looking inside. Even the smallest pinhole can let in enough water to ruin electronics.

Deck Bag

- Deckbags are specially made to be positioned atop the fore deck of your kayak.

- This is a great place to keep things you want readily accessible for sea kayaking.

- They are not suitable for whitewater boats because these kayaks have such low volume.

- Under-deck bags attach inside the cockpit under the fore deck. Keep them small so they won't interfere with your paddle stroke.

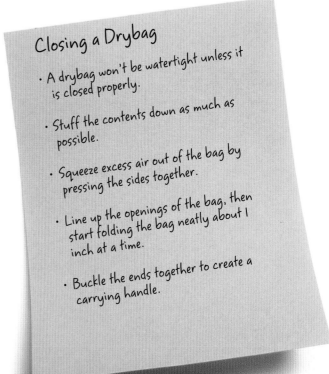

Closing a Drybag

- A drybag won't be watertight unless it is closed properly.

- Stuff the contents down as much as possible.

- Squeeze excess air out of the bag by pressing the sides together.

- Line up the openings of the bag, then start folding the bag neatly about 1 inch at a time.

- Buckle the ends together to create a carrying handle.

ACCESSORIES

SAFETY ITEMS
When you are prepared, you can expect the unexpected

You've got your boat, life jacket, paddle, spray skirt, and performance clothing. You may think you're all set to head out onto the water. But there are a few more essential items you'll need just in case.

Let's say that a rogue wave surprises you or that when you lean over to view something underwater, your boat flips over. With a few affordable items, you can get yourself back into your boat, even unassisted. You can also help rescue someone else who has capsized.

Especially if you paddle alone, you need a way to get back into your boat quickly and a way to remove water from your cockpit.

Even if you never capsize, you'll be surprised how much water gets into your cockpit after a full day of paddling.

Bilge Pump

A ring of foam provides flotation if the pump gets away.

- At some point, you will need to get excess water out of your cockpit or hatch, particularly after reentering a swamped boat.

- A handheld bilge pump is an effective and affordable tool.

- It operates by placing the pump in water, then pumping the handle up-and-down.

- Stow a large sponge in your cockpit so you can soak up the last bits of water and clean up any residual mud or sand.

Paddle Float

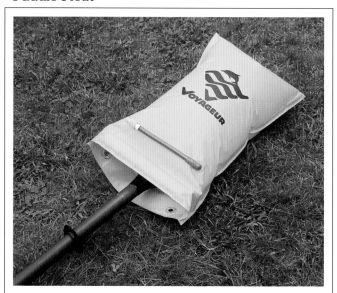

- While you are treading water beside your boat, slip the float over a paddle blade.

- Inflate both sides by blowing into the tubes.

- This forms an outrigger that will stabilize your boat so you can get back in unassisted (see page 130).

- The float can be rolled up and stowed under a bungee or alongside your seat as long as it's accessible and secure.

Pumping out that water will make your day much more comfortable.

A spare paddle is gear that experienced paddlers understand they should always carry. Paddle blades can break if stuck between rocks or roots to push off. If you flip, your paddle might float away from your boat. It could even blow out of your hands in a strong wind (this is more likely than you might think).

•••••••••••• GREEN●LIGHT ••••••••••••

Some kayakers use a paddle leash to prevent losing their paddle when they capsize, encounter a strong wind, or simply want to let go of the paddle and rest. It can be tethered via Velcro to your wrist or to your foredeck bungee. Some paddlers find that the leash inhibits their stroke. It should not be used when surfing or rolling due to the danger of its becoming entangled.

Paddle Block

- In colder climates, every second counts when you are trying to get back into your boat.

- If you paddle in cold water, you may prefer a foam block to a paddle float.

- Instead of taking the time to inflate a float, the foam block simply slips over the paddle blade to create a similar outrigger.

- The block is also useful to practice sculling and rolling.

Spare Paddle

- An extra two-piece paddle should be stowed under your stern bungees.

- It can be a less expensive model than your daily paddle.

- But remember that if you lose your everyday paddle, the spare paddle will have to get you back. So don't buy too cheaply.

- If you have a good light-weight spare paddle, you can lend it to a fatigued kayaker with a heavy paddle.

ADDITIONAL GEAR

49

TOWLINES
You can buy one or make your own

The ability to tow another kayaker is an advanced safety skill that can save an ill or injured kayaker.

Towing is not reserved for emergencies alone, however. With a towline, you can assist fatigued paddlers or boaters who find themselves in conditions beyond their ability. In a beam wind, just the weight of the line will keep a kayak from weathercocking. These boaters may not need the physical tow per se, just help in tracking in a straight line.

None of these scenarios should be attempted without first receiving instructions on towing techniques.

If you are among the more experienced paddler in a group, you should carry a towline and know how to use it properly. A good ratio is one line for every three paddlers in the group. Before launching, discuss who will do the towing if needed.

Belt Towline

- This line is stowed in a pouch that belts around your waist.

- The benefit is that you can use it with any boat you happen to be paddling or lend it to someone else in the group.

- Try to get a belt that is long enough to go around your life jacket to absorb sudden jerks.

- Be sure it has a quick-release mechanism in case you capsize or get into trouble.

Tow from the Body

- Towing from the body means you are physically connected to the rescued boat via the towline.

- A rescue belt is the most common kind of tow from the body.

- Advanced rescue PFDs come with a rescue belt.

- This is built into the life jacket and has a quick-release buckle if you need to disconnect.

- Under no conditions should you tow from your life jacket without the ability to release the towline.

Towline length can be adjusted for short contact towing or long towing. In a long tow situation, the line should extend at minimum one boat's length from the stern of your boat. A contact tow is done with a short line that keeps the rescuee's boat in contact with your own.

Tow from the Boat

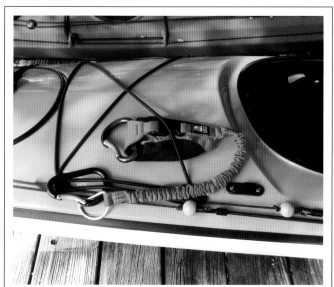

- Some people are uncomfortable with a towline attached to their body.

- You can tow from the boat by installing a U-bolt on the kayak deck behind the cockpit.

- The bolt must be within arm's reach for quick connect or disconnect. Setting it slightly off-center to your strong side will improve accessibility.

- The tow rope's quick-release shackle attaches to the bolt, and at the other end, a marine rope snap attaches to the bow toggle of the rescued boat.

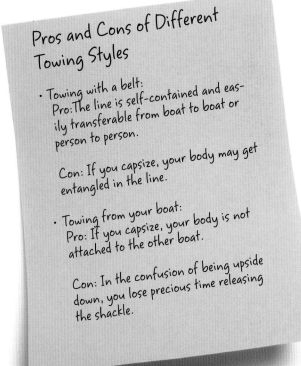

Pros and Cons of Different Towing Styles

- Towing with a belt:
  Pro: The line is self-contained and easily transferable from boat to boat or person to person.

  Con: If you capsize, your body may get entangled in the line.

- Towing from your boat:
  Pro: If you capsize, your body is not attached to the other boat.

  Con: In the confusion of being upside down, you lose precious time releasing the shackle.

ADDITIONAL GEAR

51

WHITEWATER SAFETY GEAR
Technical safety equipment for the whitewater environment

An extra paddle that breaks down for easy stowing, a first aid kit, a whistle, flares, and some duct tape: These are a few of the universal safety items that every kayaker should take on the water.

In addition, whitewater paddlers carry safety gear specially suited for the hazards of fast-moving water, rocks, and keepers, those hydraulics that trap your boat under and won't let go.

Items like rescue bags and throw bags, rescue knifes and unpin kits are items you will become familiar with as you get deeper into the sport.

A throw bag is the primary rescue tool for whitewater kayakers. It is thrown to a capsized boater who, for whatever reason, cannot swim to safety.

But because the number 1 rule of a rescue scenario is to

Throw Rope and Rescue Knife

- A throw bag is a pouch that holds a length of sturdy rope up to 70 feet long.

- A person on land throws the bag to a swimmer. As it flies, the rope unravels from the bag.

- Rescue bags feature longer lengths of thick rope.

- Having one as a backup can be handy when extracting a pinned boat.

- In the event of a tangle or entrapment, you can cut your way to escape with a rescue knife. To be effective, the knife must be in an easy-to-reach spot.

Carabiners and Pulleys

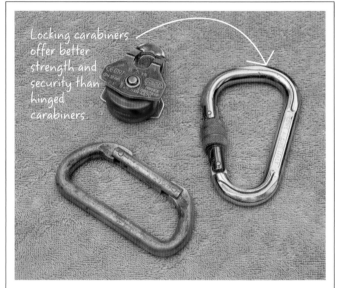

Locking carabiners offer better strength and security than hinged carabiners.

- Carabiners and pulleys are one part of an unpin kit that is used to free a boat stuck against a rock.

- The carabiners and pulleys, along with webbing and prusiks, are used to create what is known as a "Z-drag."

- You should carry two lock-ing and two hinged carabiners to set up an effective Z-drag system.

- Store the carabiners and pulleys in your life jacket for easy access. In a rescue scenario, you'll lose valuable time searching for them if stowed in a hatch or drybag.

never put yourself or the rescuee in danger, a knife goes hand in hand with a throw rope. It is your "get out of trouble" card should a rescue go bad and you need to cut away.

The unpin kit is an assembly of ropes, slings, carabiners, pulleys, and prusiks that, when set up properly, uses leverage to extract the boat.

Webbing and Prusik Cord

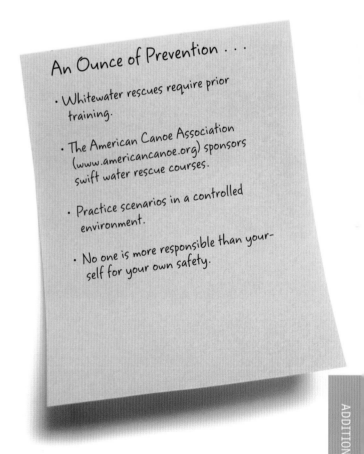

An Ounce of Prevention . . .

- Whitewater rescues require prior training.

- The American Canoe Association (www.americancanoe.org) sponsors swift water rescue courses.

- Practice scenarios in a controlled environment.

- No one is more responsible than yourself for your own safety.

- Webbing and prusik cords are another integral part of the unpin kit.

- Two lengths of 1-inch webbing, between 12 to 15 feet long, are usually recommended.

- The term prusik refers both to the loop cord made of static line and the knot used to attach it to your Z-drag setup.

- Although prusik cord comes in various thicknesses and strengths, only 5–7 millimeters is effective for an unpin kit setup.

MORE WHITEWATER ACCESSORIES
A few more items for safety and comfort

Once you've assembled the basic paddling and safety gear, turn your attention to adding some extra safety and comfort features.

Flotation is no insignificant factor when it comes to whitewater. A boat filled partially with water is unstable and unresponsive. A fully swamped boat is heavy and difficult to move.

Unless a whitewater boat has a rear hatch, it lacks the bulkheads and air space provided by a sea kayak hatch. Float bags are an effective way to fill up that empty space in the bow and stern.

The river can be a punishing place for boats. Rushing water can pin your boat against a rock. At a minimum, you'll be careening and bopping off river rocks at some time during your run.

Float Bags

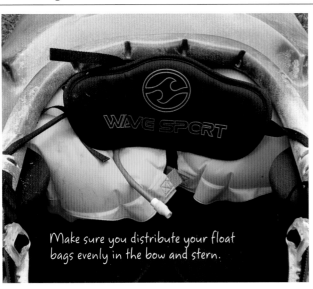

Make sure you distribute your float bags evenly in the bow and stern.

- Float bags are inflatable air bladders made of coated nylon or vinyl.

- They come in a variety of shapes and sizes to fit a variety of kayaks.

- Start by pushing them into the bow and stern of your kayak. Finish inflating the bags through a long nozzle so they fill up the space forward of your foot pegs and behind the seat.

- Routinely check your float bags to ensure they're inflated properly.

Ram Caps

- Your kayak's bow and stern are constantly banging and scraping against rocks.

- Over time the plastic may weaken and become soft. When this happens, a hole or puncture isn't far behind.

- Ram caps are plastic caps that reinforce the bow and stern.

- They can be glued on with a water-grade epoxy or bolted to the kayak.

You can reinforce certain vulnerable parts of the boat with caps and keel straps.

Outfitting your boat with extra padding and braces around the seat allows more than just comfort. It allows you to firmly anchor your lower body, making you one with the boat. J-leans and other maneuvers are much more effective.

Outfitting Foam

- Minicell is the most popular outfitting foam for kayaks. Neoprene foam is another option.

- Cut out thick wedge shapes for hip pads, back support, and thigh/knee braces.

- After cutting the foam with a handsaw, you can shave it to an exact size with finishing tools like a rasp.

- Mark where you will install the foam with a marker, then apply contact cement.

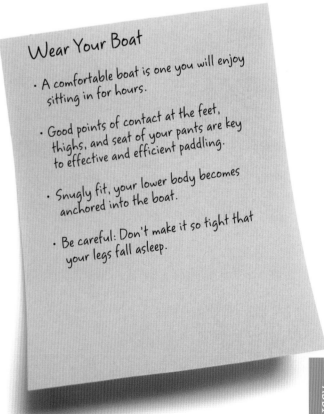

Wear Your Boat
- A comfortable boat is one you will enjoy sitting in for hours.

- Good points of contact at the feet, thighs, and seat of your pants are key to effective and efficient paddling.

- Snugly fit, your lower body becomes anchored into the boat.

- Be careful: Don't make it so tight that your legs fall asleep.

ADDITIONAL GEAR

VISIBILITY
Make yourself visible to other boaters

A sea kayak can appear very small and low in the water. From afar, you may disappear from view behind even slight swells.

You'll likely be sharing waters with sailboats, which are not very maneuverable when under sail, or Jet Skis, fishing boats, and pleasure cruisers, which can be extremely fast and unpredictable. Sad to say, you never know if the driver is paying attention, fishing, or perhaps even operating under the influence of alcohol so use caution at all times.

We've paddled through busy commercial harbors like New York and Norfolk, dodging high-speed ferries, huge container barges, and even naval vessels and cruise ships.

Legally, human-powered craft and craft under sail have the right of way. Practically, the rule of tonnage applies: We need to keep ourselves out of harm's way.

Reflective Tape

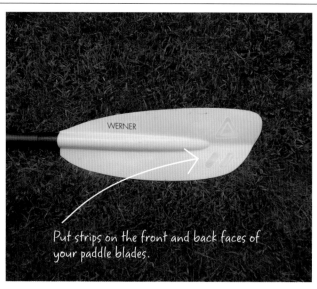

Put strips on the front and back faces of your paddle blades.

- U. S. Coast Guard marine reflective tape is available in various shapes and sizes.

- When any light hits it, the tape becomes almost fluorescent, turning an invisible boater into a moving flash.

- You can place strips above the water line along the sides of your boat.

- Some boaters even put some strips on the underside of their hulls so a capsized boat will be visible from the air.

Reflective Clothing

- Many clothing items made for boating have reflective trim on the arms and hoods.

- If not, you can add your own waterproof tape made for adhering to fabric.

- Choose bright colors for your paddling clothing and gear.

- It's fun to be color coordinated and fashionable, especially when paying a lot of money, but don't be embarrassed to look a little clownish: It's for safety!

A big part of doing that is making ourselves as visible as possible to other boaters. Reflective products, bright colors, and lights can all help. Reflective tape on moving paddle blades really grabs one's attention.

We also need to keep an ear to the weather and prepare for decreased visibility due to rain, fog, or dusk.

Reflective Deck Lines

- Deck lines should be made of cord with reflective threads of white or silver running through them.

- When light shines on these lines, the outline of your boat will become visible in the dark.

- Many boats already come with this type of deck lines.

- If not, they are fairly inexpensive to buy, and replacing your deck lines is easy.

Color

- If possible, get a brightly colored kayak that will stand out from the color of the water.

- Yellow, lime green, and orange are very visible.

- Fluorescent colors are the most visible.

- White or yellow paddle blades are more visible than black ones.

ADDITIONAL GEAR

SIGNALING
There is a variety of ways to communicate on the water

You head out on a clear morning with a couple of fairly experienced paddling buddies. The plan is laid out: a 10-mile route with a stop on an island for lunch. You'll stick together, so if you need to communicate you can just shout. No sweat, right?

Because you all are experienced, one decides to explore a creek and see where it goes. The others wait for ten, fifteen minutes and then wonder: Should we follow him, wait here,

or keep going? He's got the lunch! And the nautical chart! Two marine radios would come in very handy right now.

Every group leader should have a radio to check for inclement weather and to signal for help in an emergency. On long trips, several people should have a radio. If one person is going off on his own, he should take a radio.

Let's say you've got a long, open-water crossing. Dark clouds

Marine Radio

Always bring extra charged batteries.

- A handheld VHF radio enables you to communicate with other boaters within 5–10 miles and to call for help in an emergency.

- Weather bands (channels) give you current conditions, forecasts, and National Oceanic and Atmospheric

Administration (NOAA) warnings of dangerous weather.

- Even waterproof radios will succumb to constant saltwater exposure. Put your radio into a specially designed, clear, voice-through drybag.

Other Signals

Regularly check expiration dates on flares and dye markers.

- Flares and dye markers, smaller than a stick of deodorant, are easy to keep in your necessity drybag.

- These are most effective once help is on the way to guide people to your location.

- A small signal mirror can also be used to reflect the sun in various angles.

- All PFDs should have a whistle attached. The SOS distress signal is three short blasts, three long, and three short.

move in suddenly. The wind and chop kick up. The weaker paddlers begin to fall behind. Their voices are drowned out by the headwind. Paddlers should always stick together in situations like these, but if they don't, a whistle to signal distress or paddle signals to communicate are effective.

Flares, lights, and foghorns are other devices with which to communicate or signal for help in an emergency. Have a variety for sight and sound and various conditions.

ZOOM

Universal River Signals: Using Your Paddle as a Signaling Device

Stop: Hold the paddle horizontally above your head.

Help/Emergency: Hold the paddle vertically over your head and wave it side to side.

All Clear: Hold the paddle vertically in a stationary position.

I'm OK: Tap your head with the palm of your hand.

Lights

- You should purchase a waterproof strobe light and strap it to the shoulder of your PFD.

- With a simple twist, the strobe sends out a very strong blinking light that is a universal distress signal.

- Check the batteries periodically because this is a device you hopefully don't use often.

- Flash the SOS signal with a strong light in this sequence: three short flashes, three long flashes, three short flashes. Repeat as needed.

Foghorn

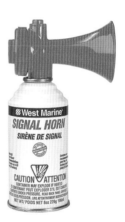

- Carry a small foghorn if conditions are right for heavy fog or if you live in an area where fog is common.

- Foghorns are relatively inexpensive, and the canisters can be replaced when they are empty.

- Check for expiration dates and have an extra canister on hand.

- Blow one blast every twenty seconds to alert boats to your presence. Blow continuously in an emergency.

ADDITIONAL GEAR

TYPES OF CARRIERS
Use the proper method for your vehicle

You've heard, maybe even seen, horror stories about a kayak or canoe flying off a moving vehicle. It's an expensive mistake, and, needless to say, a sixty-pound boat hurtling down the interstate is a deadly situation.

Boats are more apt to be damaged while being loaded and transported than while being on the water. Improper loading or tying down can cause cracks, scratches, or dents in your boat or, even worse, your car roof. Don't worry too much, however, about indentations that the rack might leave in the hull of a plastic boat. After little time in the sun, those dents usually pop out. (See Chapter 19 for details on care and repair of your kayak.)

Learn and practice how to safely secure your boat to your type of vehicle.

Foam Blocks

- These are an adequate and an inexpensive solution for carrying your kayak on top of your car.

- The blocks are usually made of minicell foam. A pair of tie-down straps secures the blocks and kayak to the car roof.

- Space the blocks so that the kayak's weight is evenly distributed.

- Take care not to run the straps through your car windows when the doors are closed.

Crossbars

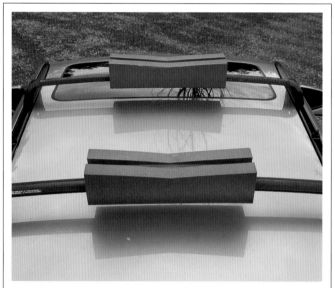

- If you have a luggage rack on your car, you can attach two crossbars (or they may already come with the rack).

- Attach foam pads to the crossbars for cushioning.

- Run two straps around the boat and around the ends of the crossbars.

- Add vertical bars to the crossbars to edge-stack multiple plastic and white-water boats.

Your options for carrying a kayak on top of your car range from the simple to the high-tech. A set of foam blocks and two sturdy tie-down straps is a simple and inexpensive system. This is a good option for plastic sea kayaks, but if you've made an investment in a composite sea kayak, you may want something that cradles and supports the boat.

Bottom line: Don't let the specter of transporting a kayak keep you from enjoying the sport. Part of the fun of this sport is visiting new places and discovering them in your boat.

YELLOW ● LIGHT

Check your vehicle's owner's manual for the load capacity of your roof and/or luggage rack before purchasing a rack system. Whether you have a roof with or without gutters will also determine the type of rack you need.

Saddle System

- Adjustable kayak saddles or J-hooks are attached to the crossbars to "cradle" your boat.

- Straps are often built in to the cradle system, making loading and unloading a breeze.

- Cradles that tilt down allow one person to more easily load a kayak.

- Thule, Yakima, and Malone are three of the more common makers of roof rack systems. Be sure to get the system that fits your car.

D.I.Y. versus Custom

- Do-it-yourself foam blocks and straps are inexpensive, and when they are not in use, there's no wind resistance.

- We do not recommend foam blocks for more expensive boats or long trips.

- Custom racks are adjustable, they cradle your boat securely, and, once installed, they are quick and easy to load.

- You'll probably spend several hundred dollars on a custom rack system.

CAR-TOP LOADING
Figure out a good system from the beginning

Once you paddle regularly, loading and unloading will become a smooth, well-choreographed routine. After the boat is loaded on our car, one of us usually ties down the straps while the other gathers the gear and throws it into the back of the car.

If you have a paddling partner, each should grab one end and lift the boat onto the roof. For many single kayakers, especially women, getting the boat onto the car by one's self is perhaps the most intimidating part of the sport.

If you do paddle with others, don't be too shy to ask for help. Having two people is the best way to quickly and efficiently get a boat onto a vehicle. Having two people reduces the risk of dropping a boat and causing damage to your boat, your car's finish, or even the windshield. Don't try to be a hero!

Two-person Load

Position one person at the bow and one at the stern.

- Bend your knees and grasp the boat with two hands firmly around the hull. Do not rely on the carrying toggles alone.

- Lift the boat up over your head; then place it carefully onto the roof rack.

- Do not let go until you check to be sure it is balanced fore and aft and won't tilt down.

- Don't underestimate the power of the wind. We've seen the wind blow an unstrapped boat off the roof more than once while the person was loading his gear.

One-person Load

You may want to place a pad or towel beneath the stern of the boat to cushion it.

- Place the boat onto the ground alongside your vehicle.

- Lift the bow and place it onto the forward crossbar or in the forward cradle.

- Without letting go of the boat, grasp the cockpit coaming with one hand; place the other underneath the hull.

- Lift the stern up into the rear cradle or crossbar.

When you get off the water, take turns helping each other carry and lift your boats; then do the tie-downs yourself. You don't want to trust this step to someone else. If someone else does it for you, be sure to test the straps.

If you do paddle alone, experiment with different lift methods. We show a few here, but there are no hard and fast rules. Find what works for you.

············ RED ● LIGHT ··············

Other than the essential, lightweight gear like paddles, spray skirts, and PFDs, never put a loaded kayak onto your car top. Not only does it add to the weight that your rack system has to hold, but also the additional weight may damage the boat's hull.

One-person Rear Load: Step 1

- Another good one-person method is to load from the rear of the car.

- Place a pad or towel under the stern of a fiberglass or Kevlar boat to protect it.

- Lift the bow and place it into the cradle or onto the crossbar.

- Be sure the bow is stable enough that it won't fall off for the next maneuver.

One-person Rear Load: Step 2

- Walk your hands down the hull to keep the boat from slipping off.

- Place a hand under the hull near the stern.

- With one motion, lift the stern up and slide the boat forward.

- Inch the boat forward until the bow rests in the proper position in the forward cradle or crossbar.

TYING DOWN
Proper and secure tie-downs are essential

Tying a boat too loosely or incorrectly to your roof can have disastrous results. But tying too tightly can damage it as well, causing dents in a plastic boat or cracks in the gel coat of a fiberglass or Kevlar boat. Never tighten to the point that the hull flexes or flattens.

Strapping down tightly around the cockpit isn't very secure and can damage the coaming. Try to run the straps fore and

aft of the cockpit and avoid any deck hardware like skeg controls. If possible, run straps in the general area of the bulkheads because this is the strongest part of the boat.

Straps of flat webbing with buckles or ratchets are far superior to rope or cord. Try to get straps specifically made for boating or automotive use. They're designed to be strong and long-lasting. Check for frays or tears in the webbing.

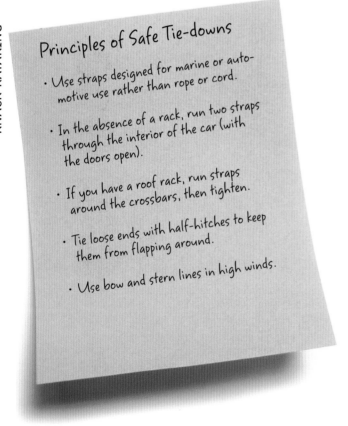

Principles of Safe Tie-downs

- Use straps designed for marine or auto-motive use rather than rope or cord.

- In the absence of a rack, run two straps through the interior of the car (with the doors open).

- If you have a roof rack, run straps around the crossbars, then tighten.

- Tie loose ends with half-hitches to keep them from flapping around.

- Use bow and stern lines in high winds.

Straps

- Straps of webbing can be purchased in a kayak shop or marine, automotive, or hardware store.

- Straps with buckles or ratchets have many benefits over rope or cord.

- The webbing lies flat on the deck of the boat, resisting slippage.

- Buckles can be ratcheted down to tighten; you don't need to perfect knots or worry about them slipping.

Frayed ends can be melted with a lighter to make them easier to slip into the buckle.

Rack-and-cradle systems with built-in straps are the easiest, although more expensive.

Upright

- To carry more than two boats on their sides, attach vertical bars to the crossbars.

- Run the straps around all boats and cinch tightly.

- Be sure the total weight of the boats does not exceed the recommended weight limit for your roof rack or vehicle. Roof racks have been known to come off in transit when overloaded.

- We don't recommend carrying more than four boats this way or carrying boats this way for long distances or at highway speeds.

Extra Lines

- When traveling in high winds, going over tall bridges or going on very long trips, you may want to add bow and stern lines to each boat.

- You can use simply rope or cord or purchase ratcheting cord with hooks on either end.

- Attach one end to each boat's bow and stern toggles.

- Hook the other end to a tow hook or similar secure spot under the car's bumper.

KNOTS
Have a few good knots in your bag of skills

Ideally you've purchased tie-down straps with buckles to attach your boat to your vehicle. But in case you forget them or need to add lines, you'll need to know a few good knots for different purposes.

Securing a kayak to the roof of your car is one task where safety is dependent on how well you tie your knots. Practice your knots and ask someone else to test them for you. And if you allow someone else to tie down your boat, always check the knots before taking off. It's your responsibility.

Some versatile knots, like the trucker's hitch and the bowline, can serve a variety of purposes and are sometimes interchangeable.

If you plan on kayak camping, there are a lot of uses for good knots, including setting up a tarp, cinching down a tent

Bowline

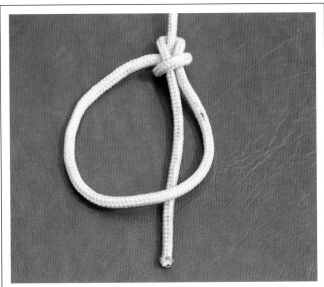

- Use this knot to attach kayaks to cars.

- Make a small loop at one end of the rope, with the shorter end of the rope over the longer end.

- Bring the shorter end up through the hole, around the longer end, and back down into the hole.

- Pull tight. No matter how much it's tightened, this knot is easy to untie.

Trucker's Hitch

- Use for bow and stern lines.

- Form an eye by twisting the rope. Pass a loop of rope through the eye.

- Pass the free end around and then up through the loop and pull tight.

- Complete the knot with two half-hitches below the loop.

fly, stringing a clothesline, and hanging a bear bag.

The trucker's hitch creates a pulley. The clove hitch is very useful around a pole to keep a tarp from slipping down.

Practice tying and untying knots for various jobs and see how they work for you. A good knot holds well but also can be taken apart easily.

Double Fisherman's Knot

You can double or triple the knot for added security.

- This knot is good for securely joining two lengths of rope together and for making a rescue sling.

- Overlap two ends of rope. Wrap one end loosely around both ropes two turns.

- Pass the end through the two loops and pull tight.

- Repeat with the other end of rope. Pull on both ropes to tighten.

Ratchets

- Straps with buckles or ratchets are very useful for tying down boats.

- Loop the excess strap end into a half-hitch or two to prevent flapping around.

- If a strap vibrates loudly at high speeds, try twisting the strap once before buckling.

- Frayed webbing can be melted with a lighter for easy pass-through.

BEYOND THE CAR
There are other methods of transport

One of our most memorable paddling trips of all time was to the Dry Tortugas National Park. This cluster of small islands 70 miles west of Key West is accessible only by private boat or high-speed ferry.

We're pretty able paddlers, but, no, we didn't paddle all the way there! With prior arrangement, we were able to take our sea kayaks on the high-speed ferry that visits the national park daily. Because we had our own sea-worthy sea kayaks, we were able to then explore the uninhabited islands on our own, snorkeling by day and camping beside the massive brick Fort Jefferson by night.

Without our own boats we would have been restricted to the one island where the ferry docks. Do check ahead for length restrictions and bring some padding.

Trailering

- Small sports cars without sufficient roofline, pickup trucks, soft-top convertibles, and campers may not be able to carry kayaks on the roof.

- If so, you may want to invest in a small trailer specifically made for kayaks.

- Such trailers are lightweight enough even for the smallest sports car, but be sure to check your owner's manual for towing limitations.

- If you want to haul a larger number of kayaks than your roof will hold, a larger trailer is an option.

Folding Kayak

- Folding kayaks pack up into a backpack or duffel bag that you can check through at the airport.

- Check the airline's restrictions. You may have to pay an oversized or overweight luggage fee plus a fee for having more than one bag.

- Folding kayaks are usually made of a canvas or nylon skin over a wood and/or aluminum frame.

- Look for features like sponsons, rudders, storage hatches, integrated spray skirts, and other seaworthy features.

Some of the world's most exciting paddling destinations can be reached only by air. The trouble is that good sea kayak rentals often are not available in those remote places. There's nothing more frustrating than having your exploration of a spectacular paddling destination hindered because all you can rent locally is a plastic sit-on-top.

You can invest in a folding kayak that can be checked at the airport like luggage, or you can carefully pack yours in bubble wrap and ship it.

ZOOM

Security: We have been in areas where we were nervous about our boats being stolen off the car at night. At motels, we try to get a first-floor room where we can pull up right to the door. When this hasn't been possible, like one time in a big city, we actually took our boats off the car and asked our hosts if we could store them in their courtyard.

Shipping

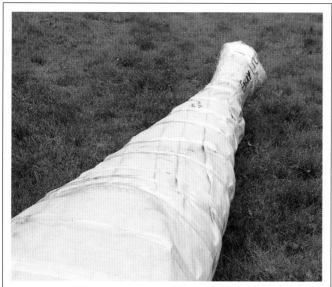

- It will probably cost a few hundred dollars, but you can ship your kayak to your destination.

- Be sure to wrap it well in plenty of bubble wrap.

- Place extra padding around the bow, stern, rudder, cockpit coaming, and any deck fittings like compass or skeg control.

- Try to take out insurance in case of damage or loss. Your boat may be covered by your homeowner's policy, but because there's usually a deductible, this coverage is useful only for more expensive boats.

Paddle Bag

- You can purchase a zippered and padded pouch to carry your paddle.

- Check the individual airline to be sure the paddle doesn't exceed the size restriction for carry-on luggage. If it does, you may have to pay an extra fee or check your paddle.

- Don't trust checking through the paddle alone. Break it down and stow it inside your suitcase, well padded with clothing.

69

GETTING TO THE WATER
Get your boats safely and easily to the launch site

Carrying kayaks, especially long, touring, or tandem boats, is always easiest with two people. But it can be done with one. The important aspect is not to damage the boat or cause yourself an injury that will impede your paddling! Don't be a hero. Ask for help and accept it when offered.

Nearly all boats come with carrying toggles at either end. We recommend also cupping the end of the boat with one hand. This will save your arm and also provide added security for fiberglass and Kevlar boats with fragile gel coats. Dropping a composite boat on a rock can cause cracks, gouges, or hairline cracks in the gel coat.

Another acceptable method that helps with heavy or loaded boats is to cup the end in a hand and place the hull on your hip to take some of the weight off your shoulder

Take-down

- Undo the straps and put them into the car so you don't lose them.

- If the wind is strong, keep a hand on the boat to keep it from blowing off.

- Just as you loaded the kayak, it's best to have two people, one at either end when you unload.

- Lift the bow and stern simultaneously and gently lower the boat to the ground.

Two-person Carry

- With one person at each end, carry the boat to the edge of the shoreline.

- You can use the carrying toggles for handles.

- However, toggles can break, and if you have an expensive fiberglass or Kevlar boat, you don't want to drop it.

- Place one hand beneath the hull for support.

socket. You should also place your free hand on the toggle just in case the boat slips.

Kayak carts are a great way to get a heavy boat to the water by yourself. Whitewater boats are relatively lightweight, so one person can easily carry them on his or her shoulder. Sea kayakers can do this, too, but be very careful turning so you don't wipe out your friend or hit a tree with your long boat!

MAKE IT EASY

Gear: At the car, toss your lightweight, essential gear (paddle, PFD, spray skirt, small ditty bag, bilge pump, and paddle float) into the cockpit before you carry it down to the water. This will save you many steps. But load heavier gear as close to the water's edge as possible, especially for multiday trips. Carrying a fully loaded boat can damage the hull and your back.

Kayak Cart

- If you're by yourself, or if you have a particularly heavy boat, like a tandem, consider a kayak cart.

- Place the bow of the kayak on the cart. The cart may come with straps for securing the boat during transport.

- Move to the back of the kayak, pick up the stern, and push the kayak and cart together.

- Folding models may be small enough to stow in a kayak hatch.

Single Carry

- Bend at your knees and grasp the side of the cockpit with two hands. Slide the boat up your legs.

- Resting the boat on your thighs, grab the other side of the cockpit.

- Roll the boat toward you and place your shoulder under the lip of the cockpit coaming.

- Straighten and balance the boat on your shoulder. If possible, grab your paddle with your free hand and head to the water.

GETTING IN
Take the time to get in and out of your boat safely and gracefully

In our experience, most capsizes occur at the launch site before people even start paddling! Being soaking wet with a bruised ego is not a fun way to start a trip.

There are many ways to get into a kayak. These ways vary, depending on your physical condition, mobility, agility, and comfort.

There are definitely wrong ways to get in, and they usually involve standing in the boat, which makes you extremely unstable. The exception is entry from a high dock, when standing for a moment in the boat is unavoidable.

We have step-by-step methods for launching, and we recommend practicing on land before getting into the water.

With the exception of a surf launch, we recommend that you put the entire boat into the water before you get in. If the

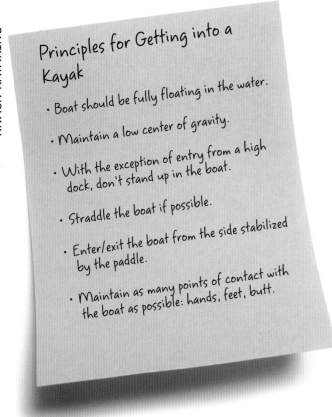

Principles for Getting into a Kayak

- Boat should be fully floating in the water.

- Maintain a low center of gravity.

- With the exception of entry from a high dock, don't stand up in the boat.

- Straddle the boat if possible.

- Enter/exit the boat from the side stabilized by the paddle.

- Maintain as many points of contact with the boat as possible: hands, feet, butt.

Step 1

- Place your kayak in shallow water. In light weather, you can have the boat parallel to shore.

- Step across the cockpit to straddle the boat, holding your paddle behind your back and perpendicular to shore.

- Squat down and rest the throat of one blade on the deck just behind the cockpit coaming.

- Most of the paddle shaft will be extended toward shore, with that blade resting in shallow water to create a brace or outrigger.

72

stern rests on land, it will make the boat unstable as you sit. Also, keep in mind that your body weight will lower the boat, possibly grounding it. Pull it out into the water a few more inches for a full float.

When possible, have another person steady the boat for you by straddling the bow or stern and putting his or her body weight on the deck.

•••••••••••• GREEN ● LIGHT ••••••••••••

Sometimes the boat is too wide, or your legs are too short to straddle a boat comfortably. In this case, enter side-saddle. Sit behind the cockpit and position legs on the side of the boat. Swing both legs over the coaming and into the cockpit and then slide into the seat.

Step 2

- While still straddling the boat, keep two hands behind you gripping the cockpit coaming and paddle shaft.

- Sit down on the deck behind the cockpit but keep some of your weight on your arms.

- First lift the outside leg into the boat cockpit. Your leg closest to shore is still in the water, bracing against the bottom.

- As you do this, lean your body weight toward the shoreline and the paddle brace.

Step 3

Reverse the steps to get out of your boat.

- Raise your inside leg—the one closest to shore—into the cockpit.

- In one smooth motion, scoot your butt down into the seat and extend your legs under the front deck.

- As you slide into the cock-pit, keep a steady brace on

the paddle. Once comfort-able, bring your paddle around and shove off.

- If you are agile and become adept at launching, you may be able to skip the brace: Simply straddle the boat and plop your butt into the seat, bringing your legs in last.

73

OTHER LAUNCH CONDITIONS
You won't always have a nice, level shoreline to launch from

When we pull up to a new launch site, it's always a pleasant surprise to see a nice, sandy beach with a gradual incline and no obstructions.

But that's not always the case in places where you want to paddle. The beach may be rocky. Sometimes you'll even have to climb over large rocks called "riprap." There may be a steep bank going down to the shoreline or a treacherous drop-off just offshore, hidden by water. Or there may be waves and surf to deal with.

Often you will launch from a concrete boat ramp, which has pros and cons. A dock offers its own set of challenges, as does launching into ocean surf.

Whitewater Launch

Have your paddle on the ground within easy reach.

- Place your boat close to shore with the bow pointed toward the water.

- Get suited up with PFD and helmet. Then sit in your boat and attach the skirt around the cockpit coaming.

- Tuck your paddle up into your armpit or rest it across your lap.

- Place your hands knuckle-side down alongside the boat. Scoot your boat into the water, grabbing your paddle on the last scoot.

Boat Ramp Launch

- Look out for powerboats that may be waiting to launch or to land.

- Have all your gear ready so that when it's your turn, you can quickly slip in and paddle out of the way.

- Bring your boat straight in, all the way below the water line so that it is fully floating, not resting on the bottom.

- Set up and get in using the paddle brace method.

74

Regardless of conditions, the principles of a safe launch remain: Keep your center of gravity low as you enter the boat; don't stand up in a boat; and be prepared to brace yourself with your paddle if you feel tippy.

If you are with a group, you can ask whether anyone has experience with the particular conditions. Otherwise, get the boats lined up near the launch site and wait until all group members have their gear ready. Talk about who will launch first and who will assist others.

ZOOM

In large groups, an experienced paddler should be the first to launch. She is on the water to assist anyone who capsizes. A second experienced paddler stays on shore and helps people launch. We don't recommend that individuals paddle off alone. By putting it in the context of safety, you send the message that a successful group trip is one in which people look out for each other's safety.

Surf Launch

- Place the boat perpendicular to the surf with the back two-thirds of the boat resting on sand.

- Set up and enter the kayak using the paddle brace method.

- Time the interval between waves breaking. Use your knuckles to scoot into the wash of a breaking wave.

- Paddle quickly to get past the line of breaking surf.

Dock Launch

- Whenever possible, kayakers should assist each other by steadying the boat either from the water or dock.

- The first person to launch can assist others by bringing his boat parallel to the launching boat and steadying it with his body weight.

- The keys are to keep your center of gravity low, do not stand up in the boat, and maintain contact with as much of the dock as possible for as long as possible.

- The next sections have more detailed directions on high- and low-dock entries.

DOCK ENTRY
Take your time for a smooth dock launch

Dock entries and exits are among the trickiest of launches even for the experienced paddler.

They take some practice to learn, and having assistance from others is always a good idea. One or two people can steady the boat from the dock while one person gets in. Or the first person to launch can then assist others by bringing her boat parallel and steadying it with her body weight.

If anyone in the group has mobility issues or is unsure, scope out the dock conditions ahead of time. Look for a low floating dock or an area without pilings that you have to lift boats over.

Think through and talk about how the launching will happen: who will launch first and how you will assist each other.

Be realistic. If the dock launch appears too risky, look around. Is there another opportunity for launching, such as a patch of

Low Dock Step 1

- If the dock is level with or below your cockpit coaming when your boat is in the water, try this entry.

- Sit down on the dock facing forward with your feet in the cockpit.

- The paddle can be used as a brace with one blade on the dock and the other behind the cockpit.

- Place one hand on the paddle shaft resting on the boat and the other hand on the shaft that's resting on the dock.

Low Dock Step 2

- Begin lowering your butt to the seat while sliding your legs forward into the cockpit

- As you transfer your weight from the dock to the kayak, make sure you lean toward the dock side, not the water side.

- As you settle into the boat, keep your hands on the paddle shaft until you are comfortable and stable.

- Bring your paddle forward and shove off.

sand or mud alongside the dock? If so, you may be better off.

Low-dock entries, where you have to drop down only a few inches, use a different technique than high-dock entries, where the drop might be several feet.

Sometimes a high-dock launch is easier if there is a ladder down to the water: Pull your cockpit up to the ladder and drop yourself in.

When assisting others, wait until they are seated stably in their boat and have their paddle ready before you give them a shove off.

MAKE IT EASY

In a shorter, plastic boat, you may be able to perfect the seal launch from a low dock. It's basically the same launch that whitewater boaters use. Place your boat near the edge of the dock, get in and put on your skirt, and have your paddle handy. Use your hands to scoot off the dock and into the water. A solid high brace maneuver is a prerequisite for this launch.

High Dock Step 1

Rest your paddle on the dock near to the boat so you can reach it after entering the kayak.

- Use this method when the dock is higher than your cockpit coaming when the boat is in water.

- Due to the height difference between dock and boat, you probably cannot use the paddle brace.

- Have two people lower and steady your boat at bow and stern (they can use their feet to stabilize the boat if it is a very high dock).

- Place your outside leg into the cockpit, positioned to the outside of the keel line. Rotate your body weight toward the dock.

High Dock Step 2

By putting your foot outside the keel line, you press the kayak against the dock, which stabilizes it.

- Begin to slide your butt off the dock, supporting your weight by leaning on your forearms.

- Slowly and carefully place your inside leg into the cockpit.

- As you lower, slide the inside foot down into the cockpit; your outside leg stays anchored, resulting in a deep knee bend.

- Settle into the seat, slide your outside leg forward to the foot peg. And don't forget to grab your paddle!

DOCK EXIT
Here's how to get out on a high dock

Getting out at a dock is a little more involved than simply reversing the steps of a dock entry. A misplaced foot could push your boat off from the dock and leave you in an awkward position.

This maneuver is inherently unstable. With a dock higher than your cockpit, you cannot use the paddle brace for stability. And because your center of gravity is so high, the odds of tipping are high, too. So use caution.

We've said elsewhere that you should never stand in your kayak. A high-dock exit turns out to be an exception to that rule. The tweak here is that even though you are standing in the boat, your weight is entirely supported by the dock.

A successful dock exit is one in which you deliberately transfer body weight from the cockpit to the dock. Do it slowly,

Dock Exit Step 1

Place the paddle on the dock or under a bungee.

- Pull your boat alongside a high dock.

- Use a tether to tie your kayak to a piling or some other part of the dock. Make sure the tethered rope has slack.

- Twist at the torso, reach up, and put your hands onto the dock.

- Draw your outside leg up into a deep knee bend and put your foot to the outside of the keel line.

Dock Exit Step 2

- Begin pulling yourself up slowly, keeping your weight toward the dockside, not the water side.

- If placed correctly, the weight on your outside foot will tilt and push the kayak up against the dock for extra bracing.

- If your outside foot is misplaced, the boat will be pushed away from the dock as you lift weight up.

- Even though you're standing in the boat, much of your weight is thrown onto the dock with your torso and arms.

thinking through your next step before you make it. Watch how others do it to see what works and what doesn't.

Do offer to assist others getting into and out of their boats. If someone pulls up to a high dock, you can bring your boat alongside of theirs to steady it. If you are the first one to reach a dock and can get out unassisted, move your boat and gear out of the way and be ready to help the next kayaker.

Dock Exit Step 3

- Pull yourself up onto the dock on your stomach.

- Keep at least one foot dangling down into the cockpit to keep the boat from drifting off.

- Place your palms on the dock and spin around.

- If alone, reach down and grab the cockpit coaming in preparation to lift the boat.

- If you're with another person, position yourselves at the bow and stern for a tandem lift.

Lifting the Boat

Don't grab the deck lines to lift a kayak. They may snap, or the deck fittings may pop out.

- With one person at the bow and one at the stern, reach down to grab the carrying toggles.

- Be careful to raise the boat up over any pilings that may be in the way.

- A third person may assist in the middle with an especially heavy or tandem boat.

- If you are alone, lift from the cockpit coaming. As you lift, swing the bow or stern onto the dock for support.

SURF LAUNCH
Perfect your beach launch to prevent injury

Cresting waves present their own unique set of challenges for launching. If this launch is done properly, however, there is a world of fun waiting for you beyond the surf zone.

As with all launch sites, your first step is to evaluate the conditions. How big are the waves? Are they breaking near shore or offshore? If the surf is too rough to put your boat into the water and safely get in, you will need to start from land and walk or scoot your boat in with your hands.

Find a point along the beach where the surf seems gentlest. Avoid places where there appears to be a drop-off or any obstructions like rocks or reefs.

Time the space between breaking waves. Is there enough time to enter the boat, attach your skirt, and launch before the next wave hits? If not, you should start the surf launch

Position Boat

- Get geared up and secure so you are ready to jump into action.

- Place the kayak perpendicular to oncoming waves.

- The boat should be no more than one-third into

- the water. This means the ground supports the back two-thirds of the boat.

- Your cockpit should be on solid beach or at least in the shallows where the waves lap up.

Brace and Enter

The outrigger is the part of the paddle sticking off the side of the boat.

- Enter the kayak by first straddling the cockpit. Have your paddle ready to brace if it is needed.

- Squat down and sit on the deck of the boat just behind the cockpit.

- Raise one leg and slide it into the cocpit, than the other leg. If necessary, lean on your paddle for support.

- Slide into the cockpit and attach your spray skirt. Make sure the grab loop is outside.

on solid ground, fully skirted, with paddle at the ready. Then scoot your boat forward, using your arms, until the boat is almost entirely in the water. Now you're ready.

Keep your boat perpendicular to the incoming waves and keep that paddle blade in the water at all times. Once you're floating, paddle like heck beyond that breaking surf. Watch out for waves that try to push you sideways. If that happens, a dunking usually follows.

Once you have perfected your surf launch and landing, you can have a lot of fun riding and surfing the ocean swells.

MAKE IT EASY

Launching others: In a group, line up boats perpendicular to and close to the shore. Have more experienced, stronger paddlers launch those who might have trouble scooting on their fists.

Walk Your Boat

- Stow your paddle under a front bungee within easy reach.

- Place palms, fists, or knuckles on the sand, whichever is more comfortable.

- If possible, wait for the wave's reach to partially float the boat.

- Lunge forward and push off with your hands to scoot yourself into the water.

Paddle

- Once afloat, paddle furiously to get beyond the breaking waves as soon as possible.

- At this stage, you are most vulnerable to a wave turning you sideways and possibly capsizing, a dangerous situation in shallow water.

- A blade in the water makes you more stable than a blade out of the water, so keep paddling.

- If a wave does start to turn you, use a stern rudder to correct course. (See page 108 for a description of the stern rudder.)

SURF LANDING
Learn to ride the waves

Like a surf launch, a landing in the surf zone requires good timing and fast reactions. The risk here is the kayak broaching, which means the wave turns you sideways. A flip inevitably follows. In shallow water, this carries a heightened risk of injury.

Capsizing by itself is manageable, but when you're in shallow water with waves pounding and tossing a boat loaded for a week-long trip, it's conceivable you could break a shoulder

or, worse, you could break your neck.

A surf landing begins with evaluating each kayaker's ability. An experienced paddler should land first to assist others as they come in. If you have binoculars, use this time to scan the shoreline and find the safest place to land. This might be an area where the waves are smaller.

It's imperative that you remain perpendicular to the waves

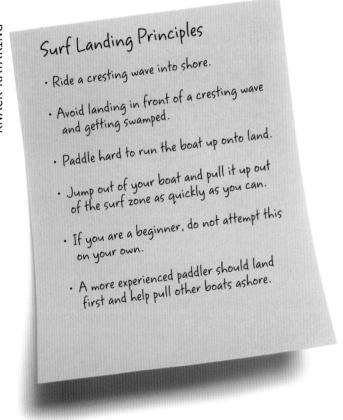

Surf Landing Principles

- Ride a cresting wave into shore.

- Avoid landing in front of a cresting wave and getting swamped.

- Paddle hard to run the boat up onto land.

- Jump out of your boat and pull it up out of the surf zone as quickly as you can.

- If you are a beginner, do not attempt this on your own.

- A more experienced paddler should land first and help pull other boats ashore.

Choose Your Wave

- If possible, choose a place on the beach where the surf seems gentlest.

- Maintain a safe distance beyond the breaking waves to study the wave sets.

- Time your approach to shore with a cresting wave.

- Point your boat perpendicular with the wave and paddle through the surf.

that push you ashore. Even a slight turn, and the wave will push you sideways and capsize

Time your landing. If you're ahead of a cresting wave, it will break over you, slamming your boat into the bottom for a very bumpy landing.

Quick reactions help once you are on land. Stow your paddle or toss it up onto the beach. Pop the skirt and jump from the boat. No points for style here: Get out and pull your boat up out of the surf as fast as you can.

Maintain Course

Never stop paddling!

- Keep paddling and let the waves drive you toward land.

- If a wave starts to turn you sideways, use a stem rudder stroke to correct your course.

- To stern rudder, rotate your torso and place the paddle

blade in the water just behind your hip.

- Push the blade away from the boat. (See page 108 for more details on executing a stem rudder.)

Quick Exit

- Ride the wave up onto the shoreline as far as you can.

- Employ speed and agility to exit the boat as quickly as possible, popping your spray skirt off by pulling the grab loop forward.

- Hold the paddle in one hand and grab the bow toggle loop with the other.

- Pull the boat up out of the surf zone to safety. If you are with a group, return to the water's edge to assist other paddlers.

HOLDING THE PADDLE
Learn the proper grip from the beginning

It sounds pretty simple: Just grab the paddle and stick it into the water.

But how you hold your paddle—your hand position and your grip—affects stroke efficiency. That in turn dictates just how tired you'll feel after a long day paddling.

A too-tight grip can lead to muscle strain or repetitive stress injuries like tendonitis or carpal tunnel. Hold the paddle as loosely as you can without letting it fly out of your hands. A relaxed grip translates into proper wrist alignment, relaxed arms, and loose shoulders, which in turn equal comfort.

Once you establish proper hand placement on the paddle shaft, check it every so often as you paddle. Trust us: Your hands will shift up and down the paddle, especially as you transition between strokes. If hand placement is uneven, you

Feathering

- Blades set at an angle from each other are considered offset, or feathered.

- Pro: Feathering reduces wind resistance because, during the forward stroke, the upper blade slices through the air. Also, the upper blade is in proper

- position for a brace move if necessary.

- Con: Paddlers tend to rotate their control, or fixed, wrist on each stroke (similar to twisting a motorcycle throttle), which may lead to wrist fatigue or a repetitive stress injury.

Grip

- Hold the paddle with two hands.

- Align knuckles with the upper (longer) edge of the paddle blade.

- On feathered paddles, the knuckles of the control, or

- fixed, hand line up with the edge of the blade. On straight blades, knuckles on both hands are aligned.

- Grip should be relaxed and loose, especially at the top of your forward stroke.

84

cannot paddle a boat in a straight line.

Although there is a right way and many wrong ways to hold a kayak paddle, there are some choices that are purely a matter of personal preference. Whether to feather the blade is one of them. Like the ongoing debate over skegs versus rudders, the pros and cons of feathered or unfeathered provide fodder for hours of debate.

Fortunately, it's easy to try out both ways and a variety of angles because most paddles are adjustable.

ZOOM

Parts of a kayak paddle: Two blades at either end of a shaft. The shaft is usually two pieces, connected in the middle by a joint, or ferrule, with a release button. Where the blade tapers to the shaft is called the "throat." The blade has a power face and a back face.

BASIC STROKES

Blade

Think of the blade as a spoon. The power face is the side that scoops the water.

- With asymmetric (Euro) paddles, the longer edge of the blade should be up and the shorter end down.

- The power (concave) face of the blades should face you.

- The back face may have a rib that adds strength to the blade.

- Some paddles have the brand name written across the blades. If you can read it right side up, the paddle blade is positioned correctly.

Hand Position

Normal setup position refers to hands properly spaced on the paddle shaft, ready for a forward stroke.

- Hold the paddle over your head, like a weightlifter holding barbells aloft. Rest the ferrule joint atop your head.

- Look at your elbows and move your hands in or out until your elbows are at right angles.

- You can position the drip-rings outside of each fist as a reminder of where your hands should go.

- Fingers, wrist, hands, and arms should be aligned. Try loosening your pinky and ring fingers to achieve proper alignment. (This also helps keep your grip loose.)

85

TOURING FORWARD STROKE
This is the most important stroke for every paddler

As its name implies, this is the stroke that moves your boat forward. The fundamentals are fairly basic, yet you may spend years perfecting them. Once you've "got it," you know it. When you hit that sweet spot, euphoria is not an exaggeration.

There are three basic elements to the forward stroke: catch, power, and recovery. They can be remembered with the familiar acronym CPR.

Mary thought she had a pretty good forward stroke until she paddled with Olympic champion Greg Barton during a clinic in the Florida Keys. In just twenty seconds, Greg diagnosed two ticks in her stroke: not fully rotating for the catch (even though Mary insisted she was) and not extending her arm fully. When she rotated and completely straightened her arm at the catch phase of the stroke, she immediately got a

Catch

Throughout the stroke, keep your shoulders relaxed and don't forget to breathe.

- Hold your paddle in normal setup position. Wind up your torso by rotating at the hips.

- As you wind up, extend that lower arm forward, as if reaching for the bow with the paddle blade.

- If your torso is fully rotated, your leg on the off-stroke side will bend slightly; your leg on the on-stroke side is fully extended, and the foot is pressed firmly on the foot peg.

- Catch the water by plunging the blade in up to the throat.

Power

Open your fingers slightly as you push or punch with the top hand.

- Start unwinding your torso, which in turn moves the paddle.

- Push the upper hand forward and slightly across the deck of the kayak, as if you were reading the time on a wristwatch.

- Resist pulling with the bottom arm. Keep telling yourself to "push, don't pull."

- As you stroke, you can bicycle your legs to add power.

bigger bite out of the power stroke.

There are many schools of thought and methods of teaching the forward stroke. What all techniques have in common is one unalterable principle: rotation.

Lots of people think you need to have upper-body strength, especially in the arms, to paddle well. If you're using your arms, you're not doing it right. The forward stroke involves the entire body, but mostly the core or torso, like Pilates. These muscles are much stronger than the arms alone.

ZOOM

In the descriptions of strokes and maneuvers that follow, you'll notice that we repeat ourselves. There's a reason for this repetition. Slow, deliberate action at the start of every stroke focuses your attention. By focusing on hand position on the paddle and a proper torso rotation, you ensure that the steps that follow will flow.

BASIC STROKES

Recovery

The length of a forward stroke is actually short: toe to hip.

- Lift the paddle from the water when it comes even with your hip.

- You should now be fully rotated in the opposite direction, ready for a catch on the opposite side.

- Your lower arm should be fully extended.

- If you use a feathered paddle, proper recovery technique puts the opposite blade in catch position with minimal wrist movement.

High Angle

Normal setup position refers to hands properly spaced on the paddle shaft, ready for a forward stroke.

- The previous three photos showed a low-angle touring stroke good for long-distance paddling.

- Notice the high-angle paddle stroke pictured here: The top hand rises above the head.

- The blade dips deeper into the water for more bite, and the shaft is nearly vertical.

- Pump your legs for even more momentum.

- This technique is useful when you need to gain speed quickly or are paddling into a strong headwind.

STOP/BACKWARD STROKE
Use this stroke to slow down or back up

So you're cruising along, deeply Zen with your forward stroke, when you blow past the turn-off for a creek. Or perhaps you've pulled ahead of your friends when a rescue whistle signals a capsize behind you.

Now's a good time for a backstroke that will stop the boat and take you in reverse.

Simply lifting your paddle out of the water won't accomplish much. Momentum keeps that boat moving forward at a good clip in the wrong direction.

A quick series of backstrokes is the equivalent of putting on the brakes. In a rescue situation, backstrokes can oftentimes get you to the scene more quickly than turning. They can also be used to position your boat for a rescue.

A backstroke is also valuable when surfing in a sea kayak.

Set Up

Power

A slap with the paddle blade is a handy reminder to keep it flat to the water.

Set Up

- Hold your paddle in normal setup position. Wind up your torso by rotating so you're facing off the side of your boat.

- In this position, hold the paddle shaft parallel to the boat. Keep your elbows up.

- The back face of the blade is about to rest on the surface of the water, behind the cockpit.

- As you position the paddle blade, follow it with your eyes. This helps rotation, and you can quickly glance behind you to see if the way is clear.

Power

- With your back hand, push the blade down into the water with firm force.

- Submerge the blade just beyond the throat.

- Push down and forward along the side of the boat. As you do, unwind your torso.

- This is a quick, firm movement. Make it smooth: Try to minimize splashing.

As waves swell and crest, you maintain your position by paddling backward.

This maneuver can also keep you in a holding pattern if you are in a current or need to wait for a slower paddler.

Oh, and don't forget to look behind you so that you don't bump into another paddler.

MAKE IT EASY

As with the forward stroke, rotation is key. This time you're winding up backward. It's a technique you'll want to practice to improve your flexibility and finesse. With very little effort you'll be able to back up, turn while backing, and come to a graceful stop.

Recovery

The length of a forward stroke is actually short: toe to hip.

- Bring the blade out of the water near the hip.

- To stop, you don't need to push the blade any farther than the hip.

- If you continue this stroke forward of the hip, you will notice that the boat will start to turn.

- Bring the paddle blade out quickly and completely rotate to the other side for the next stroke.

Repeat

- Rotate fully to the other side of the boat, again looking backward to be sure you are clear.

- To come to a quick stop, repeat the stroke several times on alternating sides in quick succession.

- For a graceful and smooth backup, repeat the strokes more slowly and smoothly.

- To turn while backing up, feather the blade slightly and angle the stroke off the side of the boat.

BASIC STROKES

89

FORWARD SWEEP
The sweep stroke helps turn your boat

Using a combination of edging and a wide, arcing stroke, paddlers can turn their flatwater kayaks gracefully with what is called the "sweep stroke."

Rather than moving back and alongside the boat, as with a forward stroke, the sweep stroke arcs away from the boat. While coaching other paddlers, we describe it like drawing a rainbow off the front of your kayak.

When you sweep on the right side, the bow of the kayak will turn left. When you sweep on the left, the bow will turn right.

In a long sea kayak, it may take several strokes on the same side—or a combination of forward and reverse sweeps—to execute a turn. Whitewater kayaks, being shorter and suited for fast-moving currents, take a slightly different tack with the forward sweep. In this case, you set up in much the same

Principles of the Forward Sweep

- The sweep motion moves the bow.

- The draw to the hip moves the stern.

- Edge your boat for tighter turns.

- Follow your paddle blade with your eyes.

- Use the full range of the stroke, from toe to hip.

- Strive for a quiet paddle, splashing as little as possible.

Catch

- Hold the paddle in normal setup position. Wind up your torso by rotating at the hips.

- Fully extend the lower arm as you reach forward with the paddle. Your on-side leg is fully extended; your off-side leg is slightly bent.

- Plunge the blade into the water near your toes. The power face is toward you.

- Remember good posture. Lean forward as if grabbing something at the bow. Keep your shoulders relaxed and breathe throughout the stroke.

fashion. But because of the current, this move feels more like planting the paddle. It's the boat that moves around the paddle. The effect is immediate and dynamic, in part because the boat is shorter and designed for quick turning.

As you get more comfortable in your boat, you'll want to add some edging to your sweep stroke. Edging lessens the boat's waterline, thus lessening the resistance of water to the turn.

ZOOM

In a touring kayak, a forward sweep has two distinct parts: the arcing sweep and a draw to the hip. The sweep moves the bow of the boat, whereas the draw moves the stern. Play around with "wagging your tail," pushing the blade in and out from your hip to see how effectively the draw moves your stern.

Sweep

The outer arm should fully extend as it sweeps away from the boat.

- Sweep the paddle blade away from the boat in a wide arc.

- As you sweep, edge the boat slightly by cocking your hip. The edge starts out gentle but deepens as the paddle moves farther away from the boat.

- Remember: Keep your head centered over the boat to keep from losing your balance.

- The sweep stroke should be smooth and graceful, with minimal water noise.

Draw to the Hip

- Finish the sweep with a final oomph of power.

- When the blade is opposite your hip, pull the power face of the blade strongly to the boat just behind your hip.

- Beginners have a tendency as they draw to let their upper hand rise above eye level.

- Concentrate on keeping your upper arm at chin level. Practice this slowly at first.

REVERSE SWEEP

This stroke moves the stern of the boat quickly

Because it can take several forward sweeps to turn a boat, paddlers often combine a forward stroke with a reverse sweep. Used in combination, the two can practically turn the boat on a dime.

As with most strokes, the effectiveness of a reverse sweep begins with torso rotation. The more you rotate, the more impact the sweep will have.

A reverse sweep is what we call "true steering." If you do one on the right, the boat turns right. If you do one on the left, it turns left.

A reverse sweep will also slow your forward momentum quite a bit, whereas a forward stroke will keep you moving forward. For this reason, the reverse sweep is excellent to use when you are in tight quarters or when you need to stop and

Set Up

- Hold the paddle in normal setup position. Wind up your torso by rotating at your hips so you're facing off the side of the boat.

- Hold the paddle shaft parallel to the boat, elbows up, knuckles down.

- The back face of the blade is about to rest on the surface of the water near the hull and behind your hip.

- This is almost identical to the setup for the backstroke.

Angle the Blade

- With the backstroke, you place the blade flat on the water and push down.

- For a reverse sweep, feather the blade down and away from the boat to about 45 degrees.

- Push the blade firmly away from the boat in a wide sweeping motion.

- Begin to edge the boat as you sweep.

turn around at the same time.

Be sure to fully rotate and look behind you before planting your blade in the water. This setup is very similar to the setup for the back stroke, but here you feather the blade away from the boat, rather than placing it flat on the water.

Sweep

The blade should be fully submerged for maximum power.

- Swing the paddle away from the boat in a wide arc.

- Bring the paddle blade all the way to your toes, even reaching forward with your torso for full extension.

- As with the forward sweep, avoid splashy turbulence as your paddle moves through the water.

- Make the move slow and graceful and remember to breathe.

Recovery

- Lift your paddle up and quickly transfer it to the other side of the boat.

- Begin a forward sweep to complete the turn.

- Repeat these steps as necessary to turn in the direction you want to go.

- You can also perform several reverse sweeps on the same side to turn more dramatically.

STATIONARY SIDE DRAW
With some practice, it's easy to move your boat sideways

Your progression through the basic strokes has given you a skill set for moving forward and backward and for turning. But what if you need to go sideways?

The draw stroke is the answer. It is handy if you need to sidle up to a dock or to pull next to a fellow paddler's boat to share lunch or open his hatch. It's called a "stationary draw" because you start from an at-rest position. The bow draw and stern draw, described in the next section, are more dynamic.

There are two styles of the draw. A draw to the hip is a rhythmic stroke that when done properly can be timed to a cadence of a four-beat dance step: one-two-three-four. A sculling draw is one that some paddlers liken to spreading peanut butter with your paddle. We cover it in more depth on page 104.

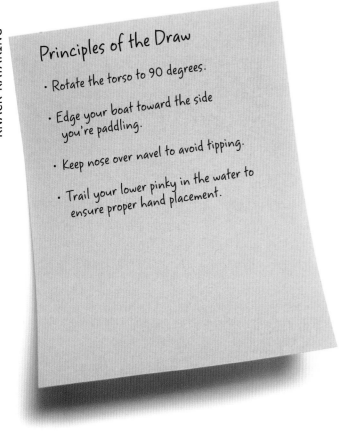

Principles of the Draw

- Rotate the torso to 90 degrees.

- Edge your boat toward the side you're paddling.

- Keep nose over navel to avoid tipping.

- Trail your lower pinky in the water to ensure proper hand placement.

Catch

- Hold the paddle in normal setup position. Wind up your torso by rotating at the hips so you are facing the object you want to approach.

- Extend the paddle out over the water.

- Plant the lower blade in the water, power face toward you.

- The blade should sink until your lower hand is at water level. The upper hand is between chin and eye level.

94

A draw to the hip is good if you are in calm waters or if you need to pull next to an object like a dock. The sculling draw is preferred in rougher water, in part because sculling itself is a form of bracing and offers better insurance against tipping. (For an explanation of sculling and braces, see Chapter 9.)

The goal of a draw stroke is to evenly move the boat sideways. Experiment with moving your paddle more forward or more backward until you find that sweet spot where the entire boat moves sideways evenly.

ZOOM

Add a little rhythm to your stoke. The draw to the hip is broken into four steps that can be timed as four beats, as in a dance step. After you plant the paddle, you draw (one), feather (two), slice (three), feather (four). As you fall into a rhythm of draw, feather, slice, feather, count off the moves as one, two, three, four.

BASIC STROKES

Power

- Using your lower hand, draw the paddle toward the kayak, keeping the shaft nearly vertical.

- Your upper hand should stay at chin to eye level and remain stationary.

- Move the paddle with your lower hand and trail your lower hand's pinky finger as a reminder of its proper position.

- As you draw, edge the boat toward the side you are stroking to help propel it sideways.

Recovery

Be sure the blade does not slip underneath the hull, or you will flip over.

- The blade is now close to the side of the boat.

- Feather the paddle so the blade that is in the water is turned perpendicular to the boat.

- Push the lower hand away from the boat so that the blade slices easily through the water.

- After reaching full extension with the lower arm, feather the paddle so the blade's power face is toward you. Repeat the draw toward you again.

BOW & STERN DRAWS
Use strong strokes for fast-moving water

Whitewater paddlers often need to make sharp, fast turns. To do so, they have the usual complement of sweeps and forward and reverse strokes. But they also have some extra weapons in their stroke arsenal. Two of the most fundamental are the bow draw and stern draw.

Besides being a reliable roll, a solid draw stroke is a must-have skill for river runners. It is a building block for learning and making more advanced maneuvers.

At the least, a bow draw helps you grab eddies, those all-important slack water spots on the river. Eddies are a place to rest or to gather with other boaters and assess what's next downriver. When it's time to move on, the bow draw or a variation of it is used to peel out of the eddy back into the current.

Bow Draw Catch

Feather the paddle blade slightly toward the bow.

- Hold the paddle in normal setup position. Wind up the torso by rotating at the hips so you are facing off the side of the boat.

- Reach the paddle out off the side of the boat. The blade's power face is toward you and feathered to the bow.

- Your upper hand is above your head. Your lower hand is near the surface of the water.

- Plant the paddle in the water.

Bow Draw Power

- Begin to move the paddle toward the bow by unwinding your torso.

- Edge the boat toward the side you're stroking.

- Keep the paddle shaft vertical to the water or nearly so.

- Follow the blade with your head.

If you need to turn quickly, a combination of a high brace, bow draw, and forward stroke carves a tight turn.

A stern draw, by contrast, produces a wider turn. A paddler who wants to angle his boat more across the stream, possibly to ferry across and catch an eddy on the other side, would choose a stern draw as he peeled out.

It's important to remember the distinction between a stationary draw and a bow or stern draw. With the first, the boat is still, and you initiate sideways motion.

With a bow draw and stern draw, the kayak is in motion (headed downriver with the current), and the goal is a much more dramatic, emphatic move that changes your direction of travel.

Stern Draw Catch

Feather the paddle blade slightly to the stern.

- Hold the paddle in normal setup position. Wind up your torso by rotating at the hips so you are facing off the side of the boat.

- Reach the paddle out over the side of the boat.

- The angle of the paddle is lower than with a bow draw. This means the upper arm is not fully extended out over the side of the boat.

- Plunge the blade into the water.

Stern Draw Power

- Move the paddle toward the stern of the kayak.

- As you move the paddle, increase the angle of the paddle shaft.

- By increasing paddle angle, you maintain stability and get more power.

- At the end of this stroke, the paddle shaft is nearly vertical.

EDGING OR J-LEANS
Learn to set your boat on edge for more efficient maneuvers

Edging your kayak adds immeasurably to your on-water performance. On flatwater, edging makes turns tighter and more efficient. On a river or heavy seas, it is the single best way to counter the effect of current and waves that would otherwise capsize you.

When we talk about edging, we're talking a lower body movement—primarily with the hips. It helps at this point to think about Elvis and what he could do with those hips. When launching kayakers, especially first-timers, we ask them to "give me an Elvis." Basically, we're asking them to rock their hips back and forth while keeping their head and shoulders stationary.

Edging is exactly this rocking motion, but instead of rocking side to side, you rock it to one side and hold the boat there.

At the moment, it feels like you're hanging in the balance

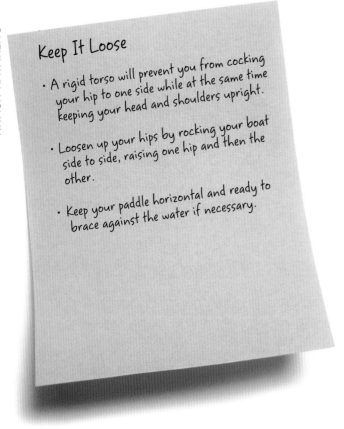

Keep It Loose

- A rigid torso will prevent you from cocking your hip to one side while at the same time keeping your head and shoulders upright.

- Loosen up your hips by rocking your boat side to side, raising one hip and then the other.

- Keep your paddle horizontal and ready to brace against the water if necessary.

Using a Dock

- Position your boat parallel to a dock that is no more than head high.

- Reach out and place one or two hands within reach of the dock.

- Cock your hip so the boat leans toward the dock. Hang there for a few moments before flicking your hip back to center position.

- If you start to capsize, stabilize yourself on the dock.

- Do this on both sides to create muscle memory in both hips.

between staying upright and flipping over.

So what stops you from going all the way over? If your hips are what moves, and your thighs are what brace and help hold the position, your upper body is upright and centered to the boat. This is critical because if your torso and head leave that centerline, and you don't know how to brace, you will flip over.

It's best to wear a spray skirt when practicing your edging. Use a stationary object, like a dock or another boat, as a safety.

Physics of edging: In sea kayaking, the less boat surface that touches the water, the faster the boat will turn. Practical uses of edging include more efficient sweeps, faster turns in rescue situations, and aids in managing powerboat wakes and breaking waves. In whitewater kayaking, edging the boat allows you to maintain stability in fast-moving, changing current.

Using Another Boat

- Find a partner to practice with.

- Position your boat perpendicular to your friend's, with their bow pointing at your hip.

- Hold their bow with one hand for stability while practicing your edging.

- Try taking your hands off the bow. It will make you less dependent on the support.

On Your Own

- Hold your paddle in the low brace position.

- Raise one hip and release the opposite knee until your boat seems to hang on edge.

- Keep your head and shoulders upright.

- If you lose balance and start to flip, slap the water with your paddle and flick your hip to right yourself.

LOW BRACE
Slap the water with the back face of your paddle for support

There won't always be a dock or a friend's boat for support when you lose your balance. These aids are handy when you first start practicing edging, but it is important that you learn bracing maneuvers as well.

The essence of a brace is the force of your paddle blade pushed flat against the water. Doing this will slow your tipping motion. Used in conjunction with a sharp hip snap, a brace will return your boat to the upright and stable position.

Another way to think of it is like this: If you were on land, just standing around, and suddenly started falling, your first instinctual move would be to reach out for support.

In a kayak, that something is the water. And the paddle blade is your hand.

Because the paddle is held low, this brace is best suited for

Position

- Hold the paddle across your cockpit about waist high.

- Your elbows are lifted and bent to form right angles, with your forearms hanging down.

- Grip the paddle shaft so your knuckles point down.

- The blade's back face is toward the water.

Slap

As you lean, flop your head to the shoulder on the bracing side.

- Lean the boat over to one side.

- As you lean, shift the paddle out over the water to the side you are tipping.

- Slap the water by pushing down hard onto the surface.

- As the flat back face of the blade hits the water, it provides resistance and your tipping motion slows

- Flick your hip to right the boat.

making minor corrections in balance or for coping with small waves. If the waves are head high, or if you've tipped over too far, it's time to call in the high brace (see a description of high braces in the next section).

If done incorrectly, this move does leave your shoulders exposed to possible injuries. Pay close attention in our descriptions to paddle setup and hand position. Nail these, then ease yourself into the motions. As your skill and confidence improve, deepen your leans for more dramatic recoveries.

ZOOM

Sweeping low brace: While underway, you can trail the back face of the blade in the water for a few seconds instead of slapping the water. This provides even more support.

Throttle

- Scoop the paddle blade forward by throttling the paddle shaft as you would the accelerator on a motorcycle.

- This action changes the blade's position from flat to perpendicular.

- You can then lift the paddle from the water with a slicing motion.

- The knuckles begin the low brace pointed down, but after you throttle the shaft, they are pointed up.

Recovery

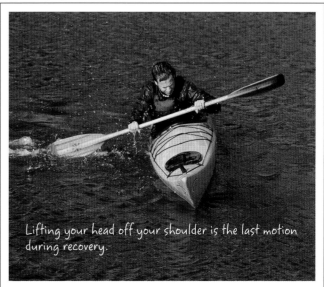

Lifting your head off your shoulder is the last motion during recovery.

- Lift the paddle blade from the water in a slicing motion.

- A vigorous hip flick has returned the boat to an upright position.

- Raise your head from the shoulder and bring it back to center.

- If you are paddling in choppy conditions, the low brace is a quick move that must be followed with a power stroke, such as paddling forward.

SCULLING
Hold an edge with a little help from your paddle

To scull, in the Old English sense of the word, is to move a boat through water with oars. Kayakers have adopted the word and the motion of the oar and adapted it for their own purpose.

At the most basic level, a sculling stroke supports a kayak when edged. It's a stabilizing stroke. The way you move the paddle is often likened to "spreading peanut butter." This is actually a very apt description. Just as you move a knife over

bread, first one way and then twisting your wrist to go the other way, so do you move the paddle smoothly through the water.

Its value lies in its being an integral part of larger maneuvers. There are sculling draws. There are sculling braces. You can scull to hold your position against a strong current or a series of waves. You can scull in a laidback position for a quick

Set Up

- Hold the paddle in the high brace setup position. Wind up your torso by rotating at the hips so you are facing off the side of the boat.

- Resist the temptation to extend the lower hand out. This exposes your shoulder to injury.

- Think of your arms, the paddle, and your torso as a single unit that moves all together.

- Keep the upper hand at chin level and the blade's power face toward you.

- Plant the lower blade into the water up to the throat.

Power

- The power of a sculling stroke does not come from pulling the blade.

- The power comes from rotating your torso.

- By rotating, you move the paddle back and forth in a figure 8 pattern.

- Think of spreading peanut butter smoothly and continuously.

rest. That same move, incidentally, will help you stay above water after a missed roll. (From personal experience, we can tell you that this last one takes a great deal of flexibility and lots of practice.)

Whatever your reason for using the stroke, you start by holding your paddle in the same setup position as the high brace. You edge the kayak, but when paddle meets water, instead of an emphatic push and hip flick, you settle into a nice, rhythmic side-to-side paddle motion. The pattern you draw on the water is like the figure 8.

Move

- Edge the boat toward the paddle so that the hull faces the direction you want to go.

- Keep the top hand firm and relatively stationary, the bottom hand continuously "spreading."

- The blade is totally submerged in the water.

- With this maneuver you can silently and elegantly pull up alongside a dock or another paddler.

Sculling Brace

Practice taking sculling one step further.

- Begin the same maneuver as the sculling draw but start moving the paddle blade toward the stern.

- Your torso will naturally begin to recline backward, and your boat will edge deeper and deeper.

- With just the slightest effort, you can even lie down on top of the water with your boat hanging on edge.

- When you're ready to get up, push down on the shaft and exert a vigorous hip flick.

FLATWATER MANEUVERS

LOW BRACE TURN UNDERWAY
A fluid turn maintains forward momentum

You've learned the basic strokes, and now it's time to put them together to do some fancy maneuvers. It's like learning the alphabet, then putting the letters together to create words and sentences.

The low brace turn underway is one of our favorites. It's fun to practice and easy to master. It's also a practical way to make a short, sharp turn in a long boat while maintaining forward momentum. The maneuver combines a low brace and a reverse sweep. The brace provides support as you edge the kayak. The reverse sweep turns the boat.

Actually, it's a little deceiving to describe the entire stroke as a reverse sweep. It's more like a bow draw. From the stern to the cockpit, your paddle acts more like a pivot around which the boat turns. Once the paddle reaches midboat just off the

Set Up

- Begin by paddling forward to build momentum.

- When you feel ready, perform a strong forward sweep on the side opposite to the direction you wish to turn.

- This forward sweep on the off-turn side is called an "initiating stroke."

- The forward sweep is described in detail in Chapter 8.

Rotate

- At the end of the initiating stroke, wind up your torso by rotating at the hips until you are facing off the side of the boat in the direction you wish to turn.

- Your paddle setup is the low brace position: paddle shaft horizontal and low, elbows up, knuckles facing down.

- Extend your on-turn side arm out over the water until it is nearly straight. Bring the blade near to the stern.

- Edge the kayak into a deep lean, relying on the low brace for stability if necessary.

cockpit, the reverse sweep kicks in as you bring the paddle to the bow for more turning power.

Moving forward at a good clip is a prerequisite for this maneuver. How you place the blade and how far you feather the blade also affect the stroke's effectiveness. Remember that this is a low brace, so you are using the back face of the blade, not the power face.

When executed correctly, the boat should turn sharply and gracefully with a minimal loss of momentum.

Low Brace

Keep your off-turn side arm tucked tightly to your torso.

- Place the blade on the surface of the water but don't slap it as you would if this were a true low brace.

- Feather the blade up so that the back face can push water as it moves.

- Lean into the brace as far as you dare and feel your boat turning beneath you.

- The blade will come slightly forward so that the shaft is at a right angle to the boat.

Recovery

- When the paddle is perpendicular to the cockpit, push the paddle forward and scoop the water.

- Flick your hip to exit the lean.

- Continue on your way by moving into a forward stroke on the off-turn side.

- It takes some practice, but once you get it, this low brace turn is like dancing across the water.

STERN RUDDER
Here's a correction stroke for whitewater and surfing

So far in this book, we've described strokes and maneuvers that fall into two broad categories: power strokes, which move you forward or back, turn your boat, or move you sideways; and support strokes such as braces that prevent you from tipping.

The stern rudder stroke falls into a third category called "correction strokes." By itself, it does not propel the boat. What it does is correct your course. It can be applied subtly for minor corrections or vigorously for sharp changes in direction.

In sea kayaks and open-water situations, the stern rudder is primarily used for surfing. Imagine a scenario where you're running downwind (you have a tailwind), and the following seas are picking up the stern of your boat. Each time that happens, there is a tendency of the boat to broach, or turn sideways. Sideways to oncoming waves is not a good situation,

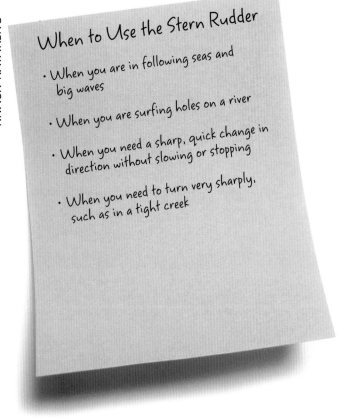

When to Use the Stern Rudder

• When you are in following seas and big waves

• When you are surfing holes on a river

• When you need a sharp, quick change in direction without slowing or stopping

• When you need to turn very sharply, such as in a tight creek

Set Up

Good rotation reduces the chance of shoulder injury.

• Hold the paddle in normal setup position. Wind up by rotating your torso at the hips so you are facing off the side of your boat.

• Hold the paddle shaft parallel to the boat. Elbows are up, and knuckles face down.

• The blade is vertical with the power face facing the boat and behind the hip.

• Plunge the blade into the water to the throat.

so you correct broaching with a slight stern rudder.

This stroke is essential for whitewater playboaters. Their whole point is riding atop waves created by rocks and other river obstructions. The currents are tugging the boat this way and that, but a strong stern rudder keeps it pointed upstream into the current and atop the waves.

The leverage for this stroke comes from two sources. You can push and pull the blade away from or toward the stern. Or for more power, you can push and pull the paddle shaft with your upper hand, like a lever.

Stern Pry

Initiate stroke motions from your core.

- Push the paddle blade away from the boat.

- Pushing will turn the boat sharply toward the side your paddle is planted.

- You can feather the blade toward or away from the stern for subtle changes in direction.

- Edge your boat toward the side your paddle is planted.

Stern Draw

- During setup, plant the paddle blade a few feet off the stern.

- Initiate the stroke by pulling the power face of the blade toward the boat.

- Pulling will turn the boat in the opposite direction that your paddle is planted.

- Alternate stern draws with stern pries to zigzag and play in your boat.

- Use your upper hand, which is close to your chest, to sweep the paddle shaft back and forth to give your pries and draws more power.

CATCH AN EDDY
Eddies are important rest and regroup spots on the river

Let's imagine that you are standing on a big rock in the middle of the river. (Or maybe you really are!) As water flows past your perch, it parts as it hits the rock. Turning downstream, you may notice that immediately behind your rock, there is a little area of calm water.

That area is called an "eddy," and it is important that whitewater kayakers know how to enter and exit eddies.

By strict definition, an eddy is a current of water that runs counter to the prevailing current. So let's return to our rock in the middle of the river. Sure enough, a closer look reveals water flowing back upstream toward you, just in that little space.

Nature abhors a vacuum, so the saying goes. In this case, the eddy is a vacuum created by the rock. Water literally flows upstream to fill it. It is a much slower current than the

The Approach

- Visually locate the eddy and determine your boat's position to it.

- Assess whether you can reach the eddy in time to enter before the current pushes you past it.

- Paddle quickly and build up speed.

- As you approach, use forward sweeps that drive the bow toward the eddy.

- Speed is important. If you're moving with the current, but not faster than the current, you will miss the eddy.

The Set Up

An eddy line is the boundary between a river's main current and an eddy's upstream current.

- Aim the bow of the kayak at the top of the eddy.

- The top of the eddy is the point closest to whatever object created it. If it's a rock, aim for the rock itself.

- A firm forward stroke puts you almost sideways to the main river current.

- Edge the kayak away from the current to prevent capsize.

downstream current, which lends it a calm water look.

How important are eddies? You could argue that a whitewater trip downriver is simply jumping from one eddy to another.

Eddies are a place to stop and regroup. There, out of the downstream current, you can rest, plot your next move, scout for another eddy, or determine the best route down the next set of rapids.

If you're new to surfing, we recommend practicing on small waves. By starting small, you can soon graduate to bigger waves with confidence.

The Catch

- As the kayak begins to cross the eddy line, prepare for a bow draw.

- Edge the boat to sharpen the turn into the eddy.

- When you plant the paddle for the bow draw, make sure you plant it in the eddy, not in the downstream current.

- The opposing currents will jerk the bow sharply upstream.

Not every eddy forms in the lee of a midstream rock. A rock pile alongside the shore creates a nice eddy. So does the inside of a sharp turn in the river. Wherever you catch the eddy, the principles never change: You need speed, good aim, and solid boat control.

Principles of Catching an Eddy

- Speed
- Proper angle
- Proper lean
- Strong stroke

PEEL OUT
When it's time to move downriver, peel out of the eddy

Peel-outs are the reverse move of an eddy turn. They take you out of an eddy back into the main current of the river.

The core principles of grabbing an eddy—speed, angle, lean—apply when peeling out as well.

Speed gives you the momentum to cross the eddy line. (The eddy line is the boundary between the two opposing currents and is often marked by turbulent water.) Setting the correct angle for crossing the eddy line impacts where you'll end up. A comfortable range is a 30- to 45-degree angle. That would entail pointing your boat out somewhere between straight upriver and straight across to the other side.

As you set your angle, evaluate your conditions. Where do you want to go when you leave the eddy? Immediately downstream? A wider angle and strong bow draw will get

The Approach

- Set your kayak so you are pointing upstream.

- Figure out where you want to cross the eddy line and at what angle.

- A low, or wide, angle will result in your kayak turning downstream almost immediately.

- If your goal is to ferry across the river, set a high, or tight, angle.

- A high angle means that when you leave the eddy, you're almost pointed straight upstream.

The Peel-out

Accelerate your kayak with strong forward strokes.

- As you cross the eddy line, prepare to feel the main current grab the bow of the kayak and turn you downstream.

- Lean the boat downstream to prevent flipping over. Use a brace or a draw stroke on the downstream side to maintain stability.

- On your first stroke as you cross the eddy line, make sure the paddle blade is planted outside the eddy line.

- When you're peeling out, the outside of the eddy line is in the main stream current.

you there. Or do you want to ferry or S-turn across the stream to another eddy on the opposite side? Keeping a higher angle to the current will help you get there. A huge factor in all of this is the strength of the current you are entering.

Proper lean is the last leg of the three-legged stool that is "speed-angle-lean." It will determine whether or not your kayak flips as you enter the main current.

Boat Angle

- If you are turning to head downstream, use a bow draw to make a hard, sharp turn.

- If your goal is to ferry across the river to another eddy, use a series of forward strokes and forward power strokes to maintain your upstream angle.

- Work in a stern draw to help maintain upstream angle.

- At some point, you can let the boat turn sideways and start setting up to catch the eddy.

Peel-out Principles

- Speed
- Proper angle
- Proper lean
- Strong strokes

S-TURNS
Eddy hop using your power and control strokes

Eddy hopping is a phrase that describes how paddlers move downstream by catching and peeling out of one eddy after another. One way they do this is by using S-turns.

The S-turn is not one particular or isolated stroke. Rather, it is a combination of your forward strokes, sweeps, and draws that helps you carve an S-shaped route down the river.

Recall that as you peel out from an eddy, your kayak is angled upstream. Crossing the eddy line, you'll feel the current take that bow and start to turn you downstream.

You counter this force with your speed and lean and your strokes. A powerful bow draw on the downstream side will turn you sharply downstream. But a series of forward sweeps, power forward strokes, and a stern draw, if necessary, will help you maintain a wider arcing turn into the current.

Catch an Eddy

- Here's a refresher: Have good speed as you approach the eddy line.

- Aim the bow of the kayak at the top of the eddy.

- As your boat starts turning, counter the current by lean-ing away. Remember: Moon the current.

- As you set up for your bow draw, be sure to plant the paddle across the eddy line, not in the downstream current.

Passing Through

- Using a bow draw, you can sharpen your turn into the eddy.

- Because you turned upstream when you entered the eddy, you're in the right setup position to peel out.

- Boat and speed control are key as you pass through the eddy.

- You don't want to crash through the eddy and out the other side before you've set the perfect angle.

At a certain critical point, however, you can give in to the current and let it sweep your bow around. Ideally you will be aiming for the top of the next eddy. Pinpointing that moment when you swing from upstream angle to downstream angle takes some experience.

Again, S-turns are a combination of strokes. So being well-grounded in how to execute each will let you focus on maintaining boat angle and direction.

Peel Out

Build up speed as you approach the eddy line.

- Here's a refresher: Set your boat's angle leaving the eddy.

- As you cross the eddy line into the current, lean the kayak downstream.

- Remember that a wider angle will likely result in your kayak turning downstream almost immediately.

- If your goal is to swing across the river, set a high angle.

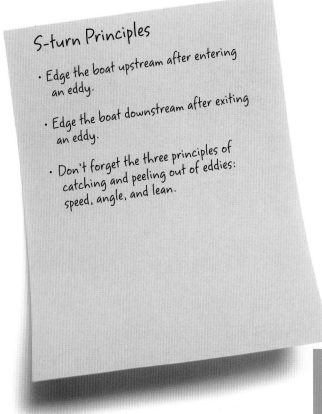

S-turn Principles

- Edge the boat upstream after entering an eddy.

- Edge the boat downstream after exiting an eddy.

- Don't forget the three principles of catching and peeling out of eddies: speed, angle, and lean.

WHITEWATER MANEUVERS

FERRYING
Move from one side of the river to the other

When you move your kayak from one shoreline to another or from one eddy to another, you are ferrying.

But wait. "How is this different from S-turns?" you might ask. S-turns take you downstream in a curving, sweeping pattern. And, in fact, you can use S-turns to make a ferry. But there are other ways to ferry.

A forward ferry is when you cross with your kayak pointed upstream. The forward power strokes and sweeps are usually used, although a good stern draw can certainly help you maintain an upstream angle.

A back ferry is when you cross the river with the bow pointed downstream. Backstrokes and stern draws are the primary tools for this type of ferry. It gives you the added advantage of being able to look downstream at what lies

Set Up

- As you prepare to peel out, point your kayak upstream.

- Set a very high angle for leaving the eddy.

- A high angle has the kayak pointed nearly upstream.

- Gain speed with firm, strong forward strokes so you can cross the eddy line.

Peel Out

- The eddy line is the boundary between the downstream current and the upstream eddy current.

- As you cross the eddy line, be prepared for the downstream current to turn your bow downstream.

- Counter the effect of the current by leaning downstream.

- Be careful that your downstream lean is not so deep that the boat turns.

ahead. In this way, you may see the line you want to take through a set of rapids.

Boat angle is all-important when you're ferrying. To underscore this point, think about the river as a clock. Your kayak pointed upstream is pointing at 12 o'clock, your kayak pointed at either shoreline is pointed at 3 o'clock or 9 o'clock, and your kayak pointed downstream is pointed at 6 o'clock.

Ferry

- For a forward ferry, maintain an upstream angle by using forward strokes and forward sweeps.

- Remember the clock: 12 o'clock is directly upstream.

- If your bow drifts past 2 o'clock, you're going to lose the ferry and swing so that you're pointed downstream.

- As you approach your destination, use the current to angle your boat for catching the next eddy.

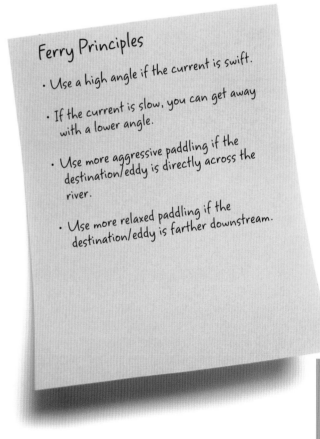

Ferry Principles

- Use a high angle if the current is swift.

- If the current is slow, you can get away with a lower angle.

- Use more aggressive paddling if the destination/eddy is directly across the river.

- Use more relaxed paddling if the destination/eddy is farther downstream.

SURFING
Learn to ride the waves by starting small

Surfing a kayak is not restricted to river environments, but the river is where the popularity of surfing has soared.

Whitewater kayakers skilled in the art of surfing have taken playboating to another level. What to the layperson looks like a paddler flailing against forces so much bigger—namely standing waves, surf, and hydraulics—is in fact a paddler dancing with some pretty powerful forces performed by some pretty skilled critters.

That said, neither Mary nor I is one of those crazy playboating critters (yet!). Whitewater surfing in the big waves is an advanced paddling skill we've dabbled in but largely left to our hotshot (and more skilled) friends.

But we've learned a few things through the years, even while taking it slow and easy on the surfing front.

High Stern Rudder

- This stroke can help keep your kayak at an upstream angle as you surf.

- It is similar to the stern rudder illustrated on page 108 but with a slightly different setup and very different paddle movements.

- The paddle blade is planted in the water near to the stern with the shaft at a steep angle.

- You feather the blade back and forth in the water to influence which direction the boat moves.

Set Up

- Rotate your body to the side you will rudder by winding up at the torso until you are facing off the side of the kayak.

- Rotation will help you place the paddle blade farther back on the stern.

- The farther back you can place the blade, the more control you will have.

- Set a high paddle angle. This means your upper hand is holding the paddle shaft around chin level.

- Both hands are over the water on the side you are ruddering.

Surfing is all about holding your kayak in a position on a wave. Although you will rely on a variety of strokes to do this, one stroke stands out. The high-angle stern rudder is a finesse stroke that can help you hold that critical upstream angle.

We illustrated a stern rudder on page 108. Like the stern rudder, this high-angle variation is a correction stroke that moves the stern of the kayak back and forth.

We illustrated a stern rudder on page 108.

Feathering

- You can influence the boat's direction by feathering the paddle blade.

- Feather the blade by rotating the paddle shaft back and forth, like you're throttling a motorcycle.

- If you feather the blade toward the kayak, the boat will turn toward the side you are ruddering on.

- If you feather the blade away from the kayak, you will turn the kayak away from the side you are ruddering on.

Stern Rudder

- If you start losing the upstream angle of your kayak while surfing, use the more aggressive stern rudder.

- Push the paddle blade away from the stern to turn the bow away from the side you are ruddering.

- Pull the blade toward the stern to turn the bow toward the side you are ruddering.

- Use the paddle shaft like a lever, pushing and pulling it back and forth with your upper hand for more powerful strokes.

119

WHITEWATER MANEUVERS

SPINNING
Use sweeps to make your kayak turn on a dime

Spinning helps you set the kayak up in the right direction. If you run a set of rapids but want to return and surf a particularly tempting wave, you can spin the kayak so you're now pointed upstream.

Sounds simple, right? Spinning truly is a sublimely simple move. But a variety of factors will influence how quickly and easily you spin the kayak.

First are the length, hull shape, and rocker of your boat. Playboats, with their planing hull and sharply inclined rocker at the bow and stern, are the quintessential spinning machines. That's what they were designed to do.

Kayak maker Liquid Logic even describes its hulls as having a patented "spin disc." (There is no moving disc on the bottom, but the hull is designed for quick spins.)

Forward Sweep

Edge the kayak away from the sweep as the blade moves to the stern.

- Wind up your torso by rotating at the hips. Plunge the blade into the water off the bow of the kayak, paddle facing toward you.

- Begin the sweep by moving the bow of the kayak toward the paddle blade.

- Lean into the sweep until the blade reaches your hips.

- Continue the sweep past your hip and all the way to the stern of the boat.

Reverse Sweep

- Wind up your torso by rotating at the hips until you are facing off the side of the boat.

- Plant the paddle blade into the water off the stern, the back face of the blade toward you. Feather the paddle so that it pushes water as you sweep.

- Sweep the boat around the paddle. Lean into the sweep until the paddle is off your hips.

- Finish the sweep by bringing the paddle around to the bow. From the hips to bow, lean away from the sweep.

If you're in a river runner or creek boat, the extra foot or two of length and reduced rocker will make you exert more power on your strokes to make the boat spin.

Current strength will impact your spin. Edging your kayak will help you spin more quickly and sharply. So having good boat control is important.

ZOOM

The essential strokes that will set you spinning off down the river are forward and reverse sweeps. However, these are not the classic sweeps illustrated in Chapter 8. The whitewater environment with its fast current comes into play here. Many times it seems that the boat is moving around the paddle, which is firmly planted in the water.

Stern Rudder

- The setup for this stroke is similar to a reverse sweep.

- Rotate, set up the paddle parallel to the boat, insert the blade at the stern, and feather the paddle blade.

- Lean into the stroke as you push the paddle away from the stern.

- You can extend this stern rudder stroke by sweeping it until the blade is off your hips.

Spinning Essentials

- The boat moves around the paddle.

- Harness the power of the current.

- Alternate forward and reverse sweeps on either side of the kayak.

- Increase your edging to make spins faster.

WET EXIT
Prepare for the inevitable

The idea of tipping over—and, more pointedly, getting stuck upside down in a kayak—terrifies people. Admittedly, it is a disorienting experience, hanging upside down in the water.

In many beginner kayak courses, a wet exit is the first on-water activity you'll do. With practice, it will make you a safer kayaker and boost your confidence. In a sea kayak, you may tackle long, open-water crossings or surf bigger waves. You may lean, or edge, the kayak with more confidence, knowing that if you go "too far," the result is predictable and manageable.

On whitewater, swimming (the end result of a wet exit) is more dangerous. Moving water can sweep you downstream. Holding on to the boat and paddle while swimming is difficult. Thus, in whitewater, a wet exit is a last resort. Better to

Set Up

Be sure the spray skirt grab loop is outside the coaming, not tucked into the cockpit.

- Cradle the paddle loosely under your armpit.

- Lean forward across the cockpit so that your forehead is touching the deck, or nearly so.

- By leaning, you protect your head from underwater hazards.

- The forward lean position is also a building block for another rescue technique—the kayak roll.

Capsize

Pounding the kayak hull with your hands alerts nearby kayakers to your capsize.

- Upside down and underwater, remain in the tucked position.

- Slap the side of the kayak with the palms of your hands to alert nearby paddlers.

- Maintain your composure. It takes less than five seconds to complete this maneuver.

- Exhale gently through your nose to stop water from filling up your sinuses.

have a bomb-proof roll (see pages 138–141).

If you wear a spray skirt, rehearse the steps of a wet exit on dry land before attempting it in the water.

Practice your first in-water wet exits in a controlled environment with others nearby. Have a friend standing in waist-deep water next to the boat for assistance as you flip.

After overcoming your initial disorientation, try hanging suspended upside down in the kayak (nose plugs would help at this stage). Strive for composure over panic, practiced routine over frantic flailing.

•••••••••••••••• RED ● LIGHT ••••••••••••••••

A successful wet exit leaves you in the water, hopefully holding on to a paddle and kayak, asking the question: What next? The answer is a successful reentry into the kayak. Wet exits and boat reentry go hand in hand. When you practice one, you should be prepared to practice the other.

Pop the Skirt

- Trace the cockpit coaming forward with your hands until it reaches the skirt grab loop.

- Grip the skirt grab loop and stretch it forward.

- By stretching the skirt forward, you begin to release it from the coaming.

- Yank down on the grab loop to release the skirt. This is called "popping the skirt."

Exit

- Release your legs from the thigh braces in the cockpit.

- Trace the coaming backward until your hands are at about hip position.

- Firmly push against the kayak to begin your exit.

- Roll out of the kayak head first. As you clear the kayak, your life jacket will help bring you to the surface. Locate your paddle if it's slipped away and hold on to your boat.

BOW RESCUE
Flip your kayak upright without a wet exit

A bow rescue is an assisted rescue in which a capsized boater uses the bow of another kayak to right himself. It's sometimes called an "Eskimo bow rescue," but by any name, it is a way you can right your kayak without a wet exit.

This rescue requires an alignment of conditions, and those conditions rarely come together simultaneously on the water. It requires that someone be nearby when you flip your kayak.

That person is aware of your capsize the moment it occurs. He or she can paddle and position the boat in a minute or less. As they do so, you have the composure to wait patiently upside down in the water, perhaps mentally reviewing your honey-do list for work around the house.

Although these conditions are rare, this fact does not diminish the value of a bow rescue. It is ideal for edging, rescue, or

Capsize

Proper hand position prevents accidental injury.

- A capsized paddler assumes the tucked position as the boat flips.

- Rather than popping the skirt, the flipped paddler extends the hands out of the water.

- Proper hand position: Place thumbs against the boat hull and stick your hands out at right angles to the boat hull.

- Wave your hands in a bow-to-stern motion.

Set Up

- The rescue kayak approaches the capsized boat from either side.

- A rescue boater can present either the bow or stern of their own kayak.

- The rescue kayak aims toward the hands that are exposed out of the water, waving.

- As you near the overturned boat, use backstrokes to slow the boat's momentum to prevent smashing into the side of the capsized kayaker's boat and hands.

rolling practice. It can also help foster good risk management and will recast the kayak in your mind as not merely a vessel for travel but also as a tool for rescues.

On a kayaking trip, paddlers should discuss various scenarios in which a capsize might occur and a bow rescue be utilized. Enter risk management: What are the conditions in which you are paddling? What are the abilities of individual paddlers? How close should kayaks stay to one another? What is the expected response in the event of a capsize?

In this rescue, both the capsized boater and the rescuer

have their roles. The capsized boater knows to take a big gulp of air and position his hands properly to receive the rescuer's bow. The rescuer should have the ability to act quickly and bring his or her boat into position perpendicular to the capsized boat.

Rescue

Rotate the boat beneath you using your hips.

- The capsized paddler's hands make contact with the bow of the rescue boat.

- Grip the bow of the rescue boat with one hand, rotate your body, and place your other hand on the bow.

- Roll the kayak up beneath you. Do not pull down on the rescuer's bow.

- Keep your head low. Make it the last part of the body that rises from the water.

Finish the Rescue

- As you surface, keep your hands on the rescue boat.

- Once upright, position the kayaks side by side.

- The rescue boater helps stabilize your boat as you regain composure and begin bailing.

- Sponge out your boat and confirm with words and eye contact that you are "rescued" and ready to move forward under your own steam.

- When ready to part, kayakers should slide boats along one another. Do not push away.

T-RESCUE
This is a fast and effective rescue

A T-rescue—also sometimes called a "boat-over-boat rescue" or a "TX rescue"—is an assisted rescue that can be a fast way to empty water from a flipped kayak. It requires two boats and is performed after the kayaker who flips has wet exited the boat.

After a capsize, the rescuer's first priority is the swimmer. Is he or she uninjured and coherent? The answer will dictate how the rescue proceeds. A disabled paddler cannot assist. If this is the case, direct him or her to hold your boat while you conduct a solo T-rescue. It is best to direct the swimmer to your bow where you can keep an eye on him or her.

If the swimmer can help, use short, clear commands when directing the rescue. Make sure that paddles are secured and that the flipped boat is within grasp, that is, not floating away.

Set Up

Stow paddles beneath deck bungees or by a paddle leash.

- Rescuer: Position your kayak perpendicular to the capsized boat.

- Grip the bow's grab handle (toggle) with one hand and place the other on the hull.

- If the swimmer can help, direct him to the stern of the capsized boat.

- Have the swimmer push down on the kayak while you lift the bow from the water. This breaks the seal from around the cockpit and raises the bow for better grip.

Raise the Boat

- Rescuer: Pull the bow of the capsized boat across your kayak. It should remain perpendicular to your kayak.

- An assisting swimmer can push the kayak as the rescuer pulls.

- Once it is across your deck, flip the kayak and drain the water.

- Alternative: You can flip the kayak upright before you drag it across your deck. The boat will be heavier because it is full of water, but it's easier to drag because of the hull shape.

At the start, the rescuer positions herself perpendicular to the flipped boat and grips the bow. In this position the two kayaks form the letter T. The rescuer will then draw the kayak across their own deck, empty the boat of water, and flip the empty boat upright.

With practice, it should take less than a minute to get the swimmer scrambling back into the empty boat.

ZOOM

A T-rescue is most effective and speedy when the flipped kayak has bulkheads (see page 16). Lifting the flipped boat from the bow position lets water run down the cockpit, hit the bulkhead behind the seat, and pour from the boat. Without bulkheads or float bags, a kayak fills entirely with water and is virtually impossible to lift.

Flip the Boat

- If you dragged the kayak upright across your deck, flip it upside down and empty the water.

- Turn the kayak upright by flipping it away from your body, not toward you.

- Slide the now-upright kayak off your deck back into the water.

- Rescuer: Use the disabled boat's grab hand and deck lines for a firm, secure grip. An empty kayak will float away faster than you can catch it.

Prepare for Reentry

- The disabled kayak is now upright in the water.

- Position the disabled boat parallel to your boat.

- Ideally, the boats will be facing opposite directions, and the rescuer can commit to the foredeck of the disabled kayak.

- Use short, clear commands as you prepare the swimmer for an assisted reentry. Direct them to the side of their kayak aft of the cockpit.

ASSISTED REENTRY
Help swimmers get back into their boat

Well-rehearsed assisted rescues are conducted quickly—and are therefore measurably safer. That's why it pays to paddle with friends who are skilled in rescues. This is especially true whenever you test your limits in unfamiliar or risky conditions.

In flatwater paddling (sea kayaks, rec touring boats), the assisted reentry flows nicely from the last stage of a T-rescue. Recall that after emptying the boat, two kayaks are upright in the water parallel and touching.

In kayak parlance, the rescuer "commits" his body to the empty boat by leaning over and hugging it with both hands to provide maximum stability.

The swimmer's job is to hoist herself onto the back deck of the kayak, a job easier described than done. Strong paddlers can kick and muscle their way up onto the back deck of the kayak.

Commit to the Boat

- Set up the rescue by placing boats parallel to one another.

- Boats should be facing in opposite directions.

- The rescuer commits her body to the disabled boat by leaning onto it and hugging the bow deck.

- The swimmer positions setup behind the cockpit and grips the coaming with her hands.

- If the reentry requires a stirrup, set this up by wrapping the rope around one boat's coaming or rigging it to a paddle.

Climb Aboard

Stay low! If you rise up after climbing onto the boat, you risk capsizing again.

- Use strong leg kicks and hoist yourself onto the back deck of the kayak.

- If you are using a stirrup, face the stern and place your foot closest to the bow into the stirrup, then climb up onto the back deck.

- Once on the back deck of the boat, remain flat on your stomach and rotate your body so your legs enter the cockpit.

Oftentimes, however, a paddler lacks the upper-body strength or is physically impeded by weight or anatomy. In these cases, you should become familiar with aids. Sea kayakers often use a stirrup to help boost themselves onto the kayak.

Reentering a kayak has to rank as one of the least-graceful moves on the water. You'll reach a point where you're lying face down, legs in the cockpit, chest resting on the back deck, oriented to the stern. From here, we coach paddlers to "flip like a seal" by rotating until they are seated in the kayak. It's never pretty, but it rarely fails.

ZOOM

A stirrup is a rigged rope or webbing with a loop tied at one end. The loop hangs in the water, and the rest is attached to your kayak or the rescuer's kayak. There are various ways of setting up a stirrup; wrapped around a coaming or a paddle is the most common. The looped end always dangles in the water. The swimmer steps up onto the kayak using the loop for leverage.

Flip Like a Seal

- The effort to climb up onto the kayak can be draining. If conditions warrant, take a minute to rest and regain strength.

- Begin to rotate your body, or "flip like a seal."

- Always rotate toward the rescue boat, never away.

- Stay low and avoid the temptation to kneel or stand in the boat.

- Work slowly and deliberately. Fast movements without prior planning often result in injuries or stress.

Complete the Rescue

- After flip-flopping over, you now find yourself seated in your kayak.

- Rescuer: Remain fully committed to the disabled boat for stability.

- The rescued boater can pump or sponge out excess water from his cockpit.

- A rescue is complete only when the rescuee is safely returned to the boat, water is pumped out, spray skirt is re-attached, and the rescued boater is stable and able to move forward on his or her own steam.

SELF-RESCUES
Rely on yourself to reenter the boat

If you're alone and flip over, the fastest and safest way to right yourself is an Eskimo roll. Failing that, a wet exit follows. The inevitable next question then is, "How do I get myself back into the kayak?"

If you're close to land and can swim the boat to shore, that may be one option. In swift water, you could swim into a nearby eddy to dump water from the kayak.

If you're a sea kayaker and carry a paddle float, you could try a float-aided reentry and roll. However, knowing the fundamentals of a roll is a prerequisite for this type of rescue.

Agile sea kayakers might be able to scurry up onto the kayak and into the cockpit in one swift motion. In the cowboy reentry you swing up onto the back deck like a cowboy swings onto a horse. Then you scooch forward and drop butt first

Prepare the Paddle Float

- After a wet exit, hold on to both paddle and boat.

- Keep your hands free by tucking the paddle under your arm and hook your leg into the cockpit of the capsized boat.

- Slide the paddle float onto the kayak blade. Secure it with a draw string or clips.

- Inflate the float until it is tight and secure over the blade.

Set Up

- Turn the kayak upright. Try lifting as you flip so water doesn't pour into the cockpit.

- Set up your paddle perpendicular to the boat. The blade with the paddle float is extended away from the boat.

- The other end of the paddle shaft is secured under back deck bungees or braced against the coaming.

- Set yourself up on the stern side of the cockpit and paddle, facing the boat. Whichever hand is closest to the cockpit grips the paddle shaft.

into the cockpit.

What works depends on conditions and your skill. If the weather is windy and stormy, the scramble or cowboy reentry is hit-and-miss. If you're offshore, you may tire quickly swimming for land.

Enter the paddle float reentry. The paddle float is a pillow-like sleeve that slips over your paddle blade. It can be inflated and, when positioned correctly, serves as an outrigger that stabilizes the kayak as you scramble aboard.

RED●LIGHT

A bomb-proof roll is practically mandatory for whitewater kayakers. Without it, every flip results in a swim. With that, there are risks of swimming, getting a foot trapped, losing gear, not to mention putting others in your party at risk as they try to rescue you. This is not to say that the most expert boater won't have to swim at some point But responsibility for rescuing yourself is part of being a responsible whitewater boater.

Climb Aboard

- Scramble onto the back deck of the kayak. Maintain your grip on the paddle and be sure it remains perpendicular to the kayak.

- Wrap your legs around the paddle shaft. In progression, swing first one leg into the cockpit, then the other.

- As you swing your legs into the cockpit, rotate on your stomach on the back deck.

- Always keep your weight shifted toward the paddle float.

Complete the Reentry

- You are now lying on your stomach on the kayak's back deck.

- Your legs are stretched straight out in the cockpit.

- Keep one arm extended down the shaft toward the

paddle float for stability and one hand gripping the paddle shaft.

- Slowly "flip like a seal" in the cockpit. As you turn, shift your hands. Hands should never lose contact with the paddle and boat.

TOWING
Help a kayaker back to shore

Mary and I were paddling on a mid-January day offshore of Florida's Big Bend coast. The horizon held an ominous sign for our trip: "marching elephants," a term for waves cast against the horizon, big enough to appear like a line of elephants waving their heads and trunks up and down. They turned out to be 5-foot waves. Winds were gale force and hitting in the stern quarter.

Faced with such conditions, I pulled out my tow rope and attached our kayaks. Its 20-foot length would keep us far apart to avoid colliding. It also gave us assurance we would not get separated. Twelve miles later we landed safely at our evening destination.

Tow ropes are an invaluable aid when faced with a disabled kayaker. That person may be sick, injured, or too tired to stay

Long Tow

Short Tow

- Boats are attached by a tow rope that is 15 to 30 feet long.

- One end is attached to the bow toggle of the disabled kayak.

- The other end attaches to the paddler, via either a tow belt or rescue belt.

- If you tow from the boat, attach the rope with a quick-release shackle to a fixture on the boat directly behind the cockpit within arm's reach.

- A short tow is handy when the distance you need to travel is short.

- It's also handy for retrieving a kayak that has drifted away after a wet exit.

- Tow rope length should be 10 feet or shorter. It can be

attached to your rescue belt on your life jacket, or by a quick release shackle to a fixture within arm's reach of your cockpit.

- Combine a short tow with a contact tow if the kayaker cannot paddle and cannot hold on to your boat.

with the group. But tow ropes can serve other purposes as well. You can tow a kayaker who needs to retrieve lost gear, like a paddle. In our case on that January day, we used the tow rope as a bit of insurance against separation.

A solo tow can be exhausting, so conserve your strength. If there are several people in the group, you can rotate towing duties (in this case, a tow belt system is almost mandatory so you can transfer the belt from one boat to another).

Assisted Contact Tow

- An assisted contact tow is necessary when an injured kayaker is completely disabled.

- This tow requires that there be a third assisting boat in the water. The assisting boat stays in contact with the disabled boat and stabilizes it.

- Attach a tow rope by linking your rope to the disabled kayak's bow toggle.

- Whether you use a short tow or long tow depends on conditions, distance to land, and the disabled boater's condition.

Principles of Safe Towing

- Have tow equipment at the ready before you start paddling.

- Carabiners or snap hooks make for quick attachment.

- Whether you tow from the body or boat, be sure you can disconnect quickly if necessary.

- If your kayak or the disabled kayak flips, disconnect the tow rig immediately.

- Towing is hard work. If he or she can, the towee should assist. If not, take your time and conserve strength.

WHITEWATER RESCUES
Have rescue strategies for swift water

Swimming at some point is a fact of life in whitewater. If you are a novice, your roll may not be reliable. Or perhaps you have a reliable roll, but you're disoriented as you rush downstream upside down.

Because of this, learning to swim is as important as learning to roll your kayak. The dangers of misreading the rapids are real and the consequences can be deadly. Foot entrapment will force you face down in the current. Drowning quickly follows. Strainers—obstacles in the water like a downed tree—let the water through, but your body is too big. You're forced beneath the water and pinned against branches.

There are different ways to swim. In Charles Walbridge and Wayne A. Sundmacher Sr.'s book, *Whitewater Rescue Manual*, they describe defensive swimming and aggressive swimming.

Self-rescue

- The Eskimo roll is the most effective form of self-rescue.

- Roll styles vary. There are the sweep roll, the C-to-C, and the stern roll.

- By whatever name, every roll incorporates the same core principles: set up properly, execute a strong hip flick, and raise the head last.

- Capsizing in rapids is disorienting. Develop reliable points of contact between your hands, paddle, and boat. Doing this will help you orient to the proper setup position regardless of conditions.

Swimming

- The safest swimming position is lying on your back, legs elevated and feet out of the water.

- This position is sometimes called "defensive swimming."

- The biggest risk in swimming is foot entrapment.

- Never stand in current and always keep your feet pointed downstream to fend off obstacles.

- Swim with your gear only when it cannot hurt you. If facing swift currents, rapids, drops, and holes, abandon the equipment in favor of protecting yourself.

Defensive swimming is when you're floating downstream on your back, legs and feet elevated. Aggressive swimming is when you are swimming on your stomach facing upstream.

As a general rule of thumb, swim defensively through big rapids. Swim aggressively when all you need is a short burst of power to reach a safe place such as an eddy.

The best rescue is one that never has to happen. We stress personal responsibility above all. If you're honest about your skills, you may decide not to run a difficult rapid.

······ RED ● LIGHT ······

If you are serious about whitewater kayaking, seek out quality instruction. Private outfitters and the American Canoe Association sponsor river rescue and swift-water rescue courses throughout the country. The advice we dispense here only scratches the surface of what you can learn. A firm foundation in safety gives you the confidence to test your limits safely.

Throw Bag

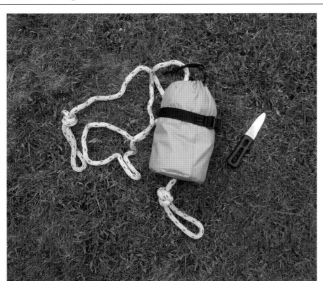

- A throw bag should be part of every whitewater kayaker's kit.

- As the thrower, position yourself onshore in an area that provides solid footing. Beware of slippery rocks or branches that might trip you.

- Grip the throw bag in the throwing hand and a length of rope in the other.

- Throw the rescue bag upstream of the swimmer so that if it misses, it will float toward the swimmer, not away.

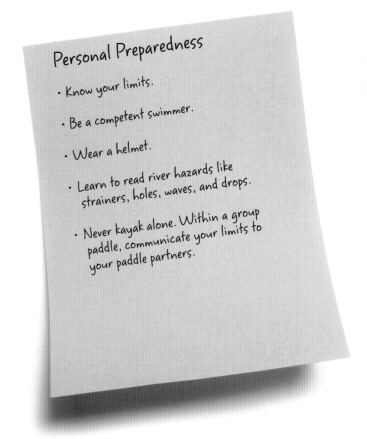

Personal Preparedness

- Know your limits.
- Be a competent swimmer.
- Wear a helmet.
- Learn to read river hazards like strainers, holes, waves, and drops.
- Never kayak alone. Within a group paddle, communicate your limits to your paddle partners.

135

PRACTICE
It's all in the hips

Your first impression when watching a kayaker perform a kayak roll might be just how effortless it appears, how fluid the motion is. That's exactly what we thought. And the truth is, after many trials and tribulations, you, too, may find rolling to be—well, not quite effortless but certainly not as difficult as our feeble first attempts were.

A good roll builds on a succession of skills. If you have not mastered the art of edging your kayak (see page 98), and you are not comfortable hanging upside down in your kayak underwater (see page 122), we recommend you review these sections.

The roll begins and ends with the hip flick. We don't literally mean that the hip flick is the first step in the process, nor is it the last. However, it is core to the maneuver. Without it, you

Shake 'Em Like Elvis

- A strong hip flick is the key to a successful roll.

- The hip flick is the same motion used to recover from deep edging or bracing.

- You are engaging your lower body—your hips, legs, and feet—in concert.

- Don't lean! Keep the upper body upright and centered as you move.

Engage Your Lower Body

- Start with a simple exercise in edging.

- Sit upright in your kayak, legs and feet braced against thigh braces and foot pegs.

- Raise your left leg so it presses against the cockpit coaming or thigh brace. The boat should tilt to the right.

- Simultaneously, press down on your right buttock and push your right foot firmly against the right foot peg. This improves stability.

- Keep your upper body, your torso, centered as you move your hips.

can't roll. Period. No exceptions.

So what is the hip flick? It is a motion using your lower body—hips, legs, and feet—to cock the boat in the water. While doing this, your upper body, the torso, remains centered and still.

How can such a movement turn a kayak upright? The truth is, the hip flick works in concert with other motions that accomplish a roll. But without a strong hip flick, the roll flounders.

ZOOM

You might think that after reading our instructions on rolling you can take the kayak out and finesse your roll. We cover some basic principles in this chapter, but nothing substitutes for hands-on instruction. Visit www.americancanoe.org for a listing of kayak instructors and a schedule of classes.

Take It to the Water

- Have a friend stand next to your kayak in waist-deep water. Her arms and hands are extended for support.

- Sit looking forward in your kayak. Reach out sideways and place your hands in your friend's.

- Edge the boat toward your friend. Continue until the boat is sideways in the water and your head is resting on your hands.

- Give a vigorous hip flick with your right hip. With practice, you should accomplish this while exerting little or no downward pressure on the supporter's hands.

Boat-assisted Hip Flick

- Set up: Kayaks are perpendicular. The support kayak's bow is aligned with the cockpit of your kayak.

- Reach out and grasp the bow of the support boat. Edge the boat to the right toward the support kayak.

- Avoid a complete flip by holding on to the support boat's bow.

- Give your right hip a vigorous hip flick. Practice rolling your kayak upright beneath you while putting minimal pressure on the support kayak's bow.

THE SWEEP ROLL—ABOVE
This smooth motion is easy on the body

The sweep roll is named for the motion that your paddle makes as you begin to turn the boat upright.

The first thing you'll want to do is establish an "off-side" and "on-side." These terms refer to the side of the kayak where you set up the roll and which side you roll up.

In our descriptions, we assume that the left side of your kayak is the off-side and that the right side is the on-side.

When we describe how to set up for the sweep roll, we are assuming you are in a controlled environment: warm water, not too deep, with an instructor, friend, or another boat at the ready to assist you. In reality, the conditions that cause a capsize will be more extreme. Perhaps you're in the surf, and a series of dumping waves has hammered you. Or you've lost it heading down a difficult stretch of rapids.

Set Up

Angle the outside edge of your forward paddle blade.

- Prepare for a roll on your right side by setting up on your left side.

- Set up by leaning forward. Pretend you're taking a bow!

- As you lean forward, hold the paddle off the left side of the kayak.

- Keep the paddle parallel to the boat with your thumbs touching the hull.

- The power face of the forward paddle blade is facing up.

- In this position, your right hand—which we'll call the "control hand"—is forward.

Capsize

Reach for the sky! The paddle must be clear of the water.

- Roll the kayak upside down by lifting your right leg against the thigh brace and leaning left.

- Now upside down in the kayak, remain in the tucked setup position.

- Keep the paddle parallel to the boat and keep your thumbs in contact with the side of the kayak.

- From your upside-down position, reach your arms skyward so the paddle is clear out of the water.

All the more important, then, that the setup position become more of a reflex than a thought-through process. Upside down in the water, eyes closed, disoriented, water flooding your nostrils, you can reestablish order by remembering the proper way to hold the paddle in the setup position. Many kayakers use hand contact with the kayak hull to reassert their sense of direction.

In a series of motions—setup, sweep, hip flick, and recovery—it is critical to remember that your head is the last part of the body to rise from the water's surface. Doing that is counterintuitive, to say the least, especially when your number 1 priority is breathing.

Hip Flick and Sweep

- Begin a hip flick by raising your right leg and pressing down on your left buttock.

- Simultaneously sweep the paddle away from the side of the kayak. The forward hand moves the paddle away from the bow in an arching pattern.

- With proper blade angle (see "Set Up"), the paddle blade skims across the top of the water.

- Resist the urge to pull down on the paddle as you sweep.

Recovery

- Finish rolling with a strong snap of your right hip.

- At the end of the sweep, the paddle is perpendicular to the boat.

- Remember to roll the boat first, lift the body last.

- Keep your head down! Pretend it is glued to your right shoulder.

- Return to an upright position with the paddle in front of you at rib-cage level, at the ready for a brace or forward stroke.

THE SWEEP ROLL—BELOW
Here's what the fishes see when you roll

A capsize is a disorienting experience. Your eyes are closed, you're upside down, and water is rushing into your nose.

This is not the time, however, to panic. Maintain composure by mentally running through a set of check-offs.

First, are you leaning forward far enough? Are your hands extended high enough that the paddle is above the water surface? Are your thumbs touching the kayak hull?

Is the paddle oriented correctly? This includes giving the paddle blade closest to the bow (nearest your right hand) a climbing edge. This means that the leading edge of the blade is tilted up. Failing to do this means the paddle will slice or dive into the water as you sweep.

With practice, the steps above will become second nature. That is the goal, especially in whitewater situations. Here the

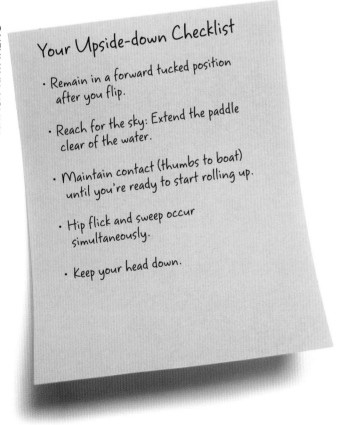

Your Upside-down Checklist

• Remain in a forward tucked position after you flip.

• Reach for the sky: Extend the paddle clear of the water.

• Maintain contact (thumbs to boat) until you're ready to start rolling up.

• Hip flick and sweep occur simultaneously.

• Keep your head down.

Capsize

• As you begin to flip over, immediately assume the tucked forward position.

• Bring the paddle parallel to the side of the boat.

• Tweak the paddle so the leading edge of the forward paddle blade is angled up.

• If you don't have nose plugs, exhale gently out of your nose to keep water from filling your nostrils.

disorientation after flipping is intensified by rushing water and hazards like rocks.

As you begin sweeping the paddle with your right hand, your torso rotates. You begin to emerge from the tucked position into a laidback position. The kayak is nearly on its side. Your right leg has engaged for a vigorous hip flick.

It is at this point that most rolls fail. The reason? The kayaker raises his or her head. It's instinctual, for sure: Who wouldn't want to get his head out of the water for a gasp of air?

By lifting your head, you lift your body. No longer are you rotating the kayak beneath you. The roll stalls halfway up, you teeter precariously and then fall back to the water.

You'll read in descriptions below a phrase that sounds silly: You should "nail your head to your shoulder." It is intended to emphasize that the head should stay in contact with your shoulder until the very last second of the roll.

Sweep

- A common impulse is to start the sweep before you start the hip flick.

- Avoid doing this by repeating (in your mind, of course): Engage the hips, engage the hips.

- As you sweep, your body unwinds from the forward tucked position to a laid-back position.

- Keep your head down until the last second of the roll! Remember: Nail your head to your shoulders.

Recovery

- From the laidback position, return to sitting upright.

- Bring the paddle back into normal setup position in front of your body.

- In real-life scenarios, a capsize may have resulted from dumping waves or other extreme conditions.

- You need to finish your roll by having the paddle ready to engage in a stroke or brace.

EXTENDED PADDLE ROLL—ABOVE
A sweep roll that offers additional support

There are a dazzling array of kayak rolls. Each has its own style and most are designed for specific situations.

The extended paddle roll fills two niches. It is useful for the beginner kayaker who may have trouble executing the traditional sweep roll.

It is also a reliable roll for sea kayakers who are paddling a fully-loaded boat or who have capsized in heavy rough seas.

The extended paddle roll shares basic techniques with the sweep roll. You execute the same sweep and torso rotation. You must have a firm, vigorous hip flick, the motion that is ultimately responsible for rolling the kayak upright.

The advantage of the extended paddle roll lies with how you position the paddle. Rather than a normal hand setup position (as with a sweep roll), instead you shift your hands

Set Up

- Prepare for a roll on your right side by setting up on your left side.

- Lean forward until your forehead is near the deck of your kayak. Pretend you're taking a bow!

- As you lean forward, swing the paddle off the left side of the kayak.

- Keep the paddle parallel to the boat, slightly submerged, with your thumbs touching the hull.

- In this position, you're right hand is forward and your left hand is back.

Capsize

Reach for the sky! The paddle should be clear of the water.

- Roll the kayak upside down by lifting your right leg against the thigh brace and leaning left.

- Remain in a tucked position. Keep the paddle parallel to the boat.

- Slide your left hand backwards until it is gripping the tip of the blade.

- At the same time, slide your right hand backwards. Try to maintain consistent distance between your right and left hands.

so they are gripping one end of the paddle. The other end is extended farther out toward the bow.

By shifting your hands, you make the paddle longer, which in turn increases leverage and helps you roll.

Beginners should be wary of relying too much on an extended paddle roll as an intermediate step. Beware there is a heightened risk for shoulder injury when executing this roll.

Ultimately, there is no substitute for possessing good technique, and knowing the right time to execute this roll.

Rotate

- Be sure that the paddle blade is flat on the surface of the water.

- Initiate the roll by sweeping the paddle away from the bow.

- As you sweep, resist the urge to extend your right arm away from your body.

- Extending the right arm increases the risk of serious shoulder injury.

- As you sweep, initiate a hip flick by raising your right leg and pressing down on your left buttock.

Recovery

- It is a hip flick, not downward pressure on the paddle, that makes a roll happen.

- If you press down too hard on your right arm, you risk tearing your shoulder muscles.

- Keep your head "nailed" to your shoulder. The head is the last part of your body to rise up from the water.

- In the recovery position, the boat is upright and you are holding the paddle in a normal setup position in front of you.

EXTENDED PADDLE ROLL—BELOW

Here's what the fishes see when you're rolling

Here are some things I think about when upside down in a kayak:

How did I get here? The answer ranges from "You did this on purpose" to "Wow, that was a big wave!"

What I'm not feeling is panic.

Rather than preparing to bail from the kayak, you should assume a tucked position and run through a series of check-offs:

Am I tucked forward enough that my helmet and PFD will protect me from underwater hazards?

Are my hands and paddle in the right position?

Is my left arm pinned to my body? Did I slide my right hand back into the proper position?

Am I exhaling gently through my nose to keep water from seeping into my nostrils?

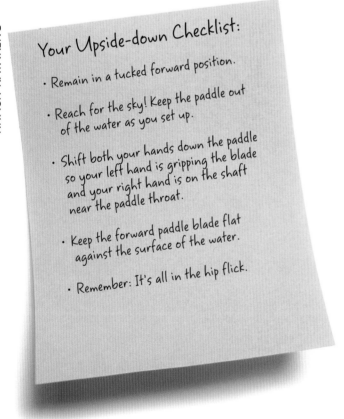

Your Upside-down Checklist:

- Remain in a tucked forward position.

- Reach for the sky! Keep the paddle out of the water as you set up.

- Shift both your hands down the paddle so your left hand is gripping the blade and your right hand is on the shaft near the paddle throat.

- Keep the forward paddle blade flat against the surface of the water.

- Remember: It's all in the hip flick.

Capsize

- As you capsize, assume the tucked forward position and hang the paddle off the left side of the boat.

- Once you are upside down, keep the paddle parallel to the boat. Reach skyward so it clears the water.

- Feel for contact points between the paddle and the boat to ensure you're paddle is positioned correctly.

- If you are not wearing nose plugs, exhale gently out of your nose to keep water from entering.

No capsize should be treated casually, but with an extended paddle roll, you certainly have options. The sweeping motion of the paddle away from the bow of the kayak is slow due to the length of the paddle. As you rise to the surface with a combination of torso rotation and hip flick, you segue nicely into the position for an extended paddle sculling brace, a position in which, if conditions warrant, you can rest and regain composure.

ZOOM

Many kayak instructors perform rolling clinics inside at local swimming schools or YMCA swimming pools. We encourage you to seek out rolling classes from instructors certified by the American Canoe Association or from qualified outfitters. Visit www.americancanoe.org or American Whitewater at www.americanwhitewater.org for more information.

Shift Your Hands

- Remain tucked forward and slide your hands down the shaft of the paddle.

- Your left hand will slide backwards until it is gripping the tip of the paddle blade.

- Your right hand will shift backwards too. Try to maintain equal distance between your hands.

- Make sure your left arm is pinned against your body.

Sweep and Snap

- Begin the roll up by sweeping the paddle away from the bow.

- Your torso will rotate as you sweep the paddle outward. Imagine you are following the sweeping paddle blade with your eyes.

- Be careful that you do not extend the right arm as you sweep. If you do, you could tear your shoulder muscles.

- As you sweep, initiate a strong hip flick by lifting your right knee and cocking your hip.

REENTER & ROLL
Save yourself after a wet exit

The reentry and roll seems at first glance so impossibly complicated that it asks the question: Why?

One answer is that if you're paddling alone, and if conditions are such that you cannot or should not complete a paddle float reentry, a reentry and roll is a fast, effective way to get upright, out of the water, and headed toward safety.

Sea kayak guru Nigel Foster, in a 1997 *Sea Kayaker Magazine*

article, compared the speeds of various rescue methods. The paddle float reentry took two minutes or more. The reentry and roll took fifteen seconds. When you are faced with cold water temperatures or rough conditions, the two minutes you spend in the water can seem an eternity and sap essential strength needed to reach safety once upright.

In a reentry and roll, you slip back into the kayak while it is

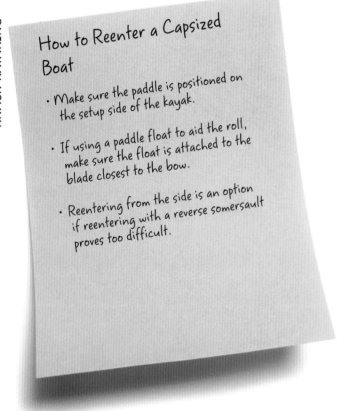

How to Reenter a Capsized Boat

- Make sure the paddle is positioned on the setup side of the kayak.

- If using a paddle float to aid the roll, make sure the float is attached to the blade closest to the bow.

- Reentering from the side is an option if reentering with a reverse somersault proves too difficult.

Set Up

- After a wet exit, maintain control of the boat and paddle.

- Set the paddle up next to the kayak. If using a paddle float, make sure the blade with the float is closest to the bow.

- If reentering from the side, face the bow of the kayak.

- If reentering with a reverse somersault, face the stern of the kayak.

upside down. Once secure in the cockpit, you proceed with the steps of a sweep or an extended paddle roll.

The very fact that you've made a wet exit adds a complicating factor. Your spray skirt is not secured around the coaming as you roll upright. This means that water will pour into the kayak, making it heavier and more unstable.

It is for this reason the extended paddle roll is especially suited for this maneuver. The extra leverage of the extended paddle will help compensate for water that weighs down the kayak.

Reenter the Kayak

- From the side: Face the bow. Tilt the kayak slightly toward you. Keep your head above water as you slide your legs into the cockpit. Grip either side of the coaming, dunk yourself under the kayak, and finish sliding your bottom into the cockpit.

- With a reverse somersault: Face the stern. Grip either side of the coaming. Tuck your legs up into a ball, lie back, and start a back flip. As you dunk and roll, slide first your legs and then your bottom into the cockpit.

Roll the Kayak

- Use either a sweep roll or an extended paddle roll described earlier in this chapter.

- Begin the roll with a powerful hip flick on your right side. Simultaneously sweep the paddle away from the side of the kayak.

- If using a paddle float, the float ensures that the blade will not dive into the water.

- Finish your roll with a strong hip flick. Keep your head down as your boat rolls up beneath you.

FIRST-AID KIT
Be prepared with a stocked kit in a waterproof drybag

A good first-aid kit is a necessity on any kayaking trip, no matter how brief. We keep ours in a drybag in our kayak at all times so we never forget it.

Choose a kit based on the size of your group, the ages and medical condition of its members, how active they are, and how long and how far away from help you tend to go.

You can customize the kit for specific needs in your group of paddlers. We added lemon-flavored oral glucose gel for treating insulin reactions after learning that a paddling buddy was diabetic. If a person in your group is allergic to bee stings, be sure that he or she carries an EpiPen and that someone knows how to use it.

Routinely familiarize yourself with items in the kit and their purpose. We pull the first-aid kit apart and repack it once a

Basic Kit

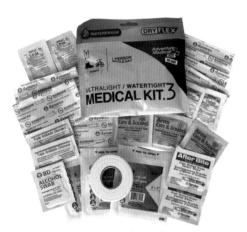

See-through zippered pouches allow you to locate items quickly.

- Adventure Medical Kits makes first-aid kits in various sizes specifically geared to water recreation.

- Or you can assemble your own kit: At the least you need gauze to stop bleeding, bandages in various sizes, latex gloves, scissors antiseptic, antibiotic ointment, and tweezers.

- Other items might include a digital thermometer, instant hot or cold pack, moleskin for blisters, sting and itch relief, and basic over-the-counter medications for pain, allergic reactions, constipation, or diarrhea.

Comprehensive Kit

Adventure Medical's Comprehensive Aquatics kit comes with its own drybag or Pelican box.

- For large groups, long trips, or forays far from help, you should have a more comprehensive kit.

- It should have larger quantities of basic first aid items like: CPR mouth guard, splints, Ace bandages, disposable syringe for irrigating wounds, medical tape, rolls of gauze, sterile wound dressings, and an emergency blanket.

- You should also add some items specifically related to water recreation, such as motion sickness pills and jellyfish sting relief.

month. We check to find out if any medication has expired. And we're familiar with where things are for quick location. Nothing is more frustrating than digging through a kit for bandages or medicine when time is of the essence.

A good first-aid kit should be considered a work-in-progress. Make a note of what others might carry in their kit and then add those items to your own when you get home.

Hypo-kit

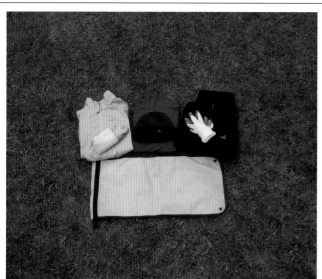

- Assemble a hypothermia kit in case someone falls into cold water.

- During cold weather, we keep the following items in a drybag in a hatch at all times: a fleece cap, long underwear (polypro, not cotton), a fleece pullover, warm socks, gloves, and a wind jacket.

- At the first signs of hypothermia (see page 156), remove wet clothing and put on dry set.

- Be aware that even in summer a drenched, fatigued paddler can become hypothermic.

Additional Items

- Any medications that have been prescribed by a physician

- Over-the-counter medications: antihistamine (like Benadryl), ibuprofen, antinausea medication (like Pepto-Bismol chewables), antidiarrheal (like Imodium)

- Hard candy or glucose gel for diabetics

- Sunscreen for sunburn relief

- Ointment relief for jellyfish or insect stings

- Snakebite kit

- Tampons

FIRST AID

WOUNDS, BURNS, & BLISTERS
Treat minor ailments before they become major

This chapter is not intended to take the place of a first aid course or even a good first aid manual. You should get both if you are going to be on the water.

Presented here are the basics for how to take care of minor injuries and how to identify and initially treat the major ones until you can get help.

Over time, we've come to see that blisters from paddling and cuts and abrasions from walking during rest stops are the most common first aid problems we face.

As minor as these seem, even the smallest breaks in the skin should be treated to prevent infection and to reduce pain.

You should also have a plan in case something more serious occurs. If anyone in your group is extremely old or young or has any preexisting conditions, even minor injuries should

When to Get Help
- Wounds that will not close and require stitches
- Severe burns
- Severe bleeding
- Bone fractures
- Loss of consciousness

Blisters

Adhering waterproof bandages on hot spots may prevent blisters from forming.

- Once a blister has formed, do not pop it unless you need to keep paddling, and it is hindering progress.

- In that case, pop it with a sterile needle and apply antibiotic ointment.

- Apply a clean waterproof bandage, padded moleskin, or gel-like dressings that cushion the skin.

- Wearing paddling gloves and using a lightweight paddle can help prevent blisters.

be taken seriously and evaluated by a professional.

Do you know: Where the nearest hospital is? How long will it take you to get to land? Does your cell phone have a strong signal? Do you have a marine radio, and do you know how to hail for help?

How to Treat Minor Wounds:
- Clean and cover even small breaks in the skin to prevent infection.
- Cool burns with water until the pain is gone.
- Clean wounds with water and dry thoroughly.
- Apply antibiotic ointment and bandage with an appropriately sized dressing.

Sunburn

- Always wear sunscreen and reapply often. A wide-brimmed hat and long sleeves are good protection.

- Severe or prolonged burning can lead to sunstroke, dehydration, and blistering.

- Move an ailing person to the shade and give her water. Sponge cold water on the skin or apply wet towels. Apply aloe vera gel or other remedy to burns.

- See a doctor if there's blistering over a large part of the body or elevated body temperature.

Serious Wounds

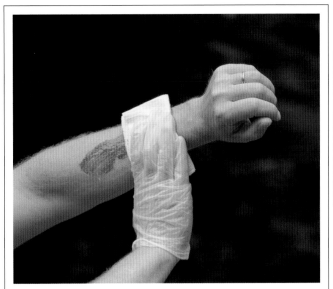

- Wear latex gloves to prevent infection.

- To slow bleeding, apply pressure with gauze pads, pushing the edges of the wound together.

- If possible, hold the wound higher than the patient's heart.

- Do not attempt to use a tourniquet or apply sutures.

- Get medical help as soon as possible. If you are on the water, you'll need to set up a contact tow (see page 132).

151

BITES & STINGS

Here are things to avoid and what to do if you encounter them

In most cases, insect and marine animal bites and stings are a temporary discomfort. However, there are some dangerous species to watch out for.

If someone is highly allergic, even a minor bee or jellyfish sting can cause anaphylactic shock, a rapidly progressing condition that can cause death.

Whenever a person is stung, always ask if they have had prior bad allergic reactions. Such reactions usually get progressively worse each time. If they carry a hypodermic kit with them, help them administer it immediately.

If you get out and walk on land, be aware of poison ivy and ticks, which can carry Lyme disease and Rocky Mountain spotted fever.

If you walk in tall grass, do tick checks of yourself, children,

Stinging Sea Creatures

The dangerous man-of-war is easily identifiable by a beautiful blue body that floats on the surface of the water.

- Encountering jellyfish in saltwater environments is quite common. The venom is located in the tentacles, which can trail several feet behind the bell-shaped body mass.

- Treat by rinsing the sting with hot water (or saltwater if hot water is unavailable).

- Some people think white vinegar works, and over-the-counter sting relief sprays are available.

- Keep watch for an allergic reaction.

- If stung by a Portuguese man-of-war, seek immediate medical attention.

Stingrays

- The stingray's barbed tail contains venom.

- Rays do not attack people. Most stings occur because people get too close.

- Do the stingray shuffle: Slide your feet walking in shallow sandy water to scare them and avoid step-ping down onto their barbs.

- A sting is very painful but usually not dangerous.

- Control any bleeding, clean the wound with soap and water, and get medical attention to remove the stinger.

and dogs. The risk of disease is greatly reduced if ticks are removed within twenty-four hours.

When swimming or snorkeling, be aware of jellyfish, stingrays, water snakes, spiny sea urchins, and, of course, sharks. Although shark attacks are rare, they can be deadly. Treat shark attacks as a serious wound and call 911 immediately.

Spiny Sea Urchins

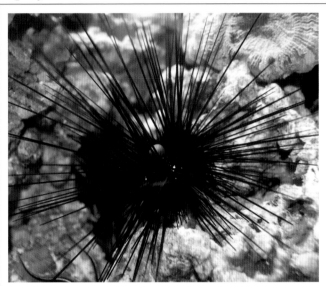

- These beautiful, black, spiny creatures can be found nestled between rocks and coral in shallow water and tidal pools.

- Be careful not to step on or touch them because the spines are painful and do contain some venom.

- Control bleeding, clean the wound, and soak in hot water to neutralize venom.

- Remove any spines that are near the surface with tweezers. For deeper spines, see a doctor.

Snakebites

- In North America, the cottonmouth, or water moccasin, is the only poisonous water snake.

- Go to the hospital if these symptoms occur after a snakebite: swelling, discoloration, blistering, or severe pain around the bite; diarrhea or nausea; convulsion, dizziness, or fainting.

- Remove anything, like jewelry, that might restrict circulation.

- Gently wash the site but do not use cold packs or tourniquets. Also, do not cut, or bleed, the bite or attempt to suck the venom out.

SPRAINS & FRACTURES
Injuries to muscles, tissue, and bones can occur even on the water

All kayakers are prone to upper-body injury, whether by suffering sudden stress, using improper technique, having freak accidents, or hitting rocks or tree limbs. For sea kayakers, a little-realized threat is simply getting in and out of the boat! Slipping on a slick concrete boat ramp or losing footing on rocks can cause serious injury, so take care and help each other when launching.

Sprains are an injury to the ligaments. Treat these with the RICE method: rest, ice, compress, and elevate.

Fractures are bone breaks. These will be obvious in the case of a compound fracture when the bone breaks through the skin. Or they could be unseen hairline fractures detectable only with X-ray.

Sometimes it's difficult to tell the difference between a sprain

RICE

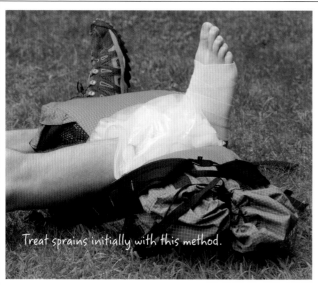

Treat sprains initially with this method.

- Rest. If you are out on the water, you may need to tow the person in his or her boat.

- Ice. Helps reduce pain and swelling. If no ice is available, use a cloth soaked in cold water or snow.

- Compress. Use gentle pressure by applying an Ace bandage.

- Elevate. If possible, raise the injury above the heart.

Wrapping Sprains

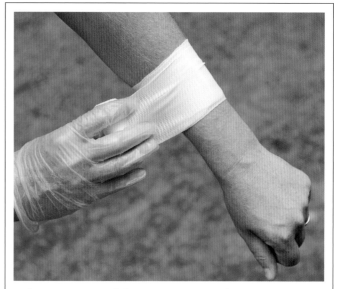

- Do not wrap so tightly as to cut off circulation.

- An elastic bandage should be applied at about half of its potential for stretching.

- Wrap a foot or wrist in a figure 8 pattern.

- If a fracture is suspected, go to the hospital.

and a fracture because both cause pain, swelling, and bruising. When in doubt, treat like a fracture to be on the safe side because moving a fractured bone can cause more damage.

Other injuries occur from overuse of muscles, improper technique, or just plain fatigue. Overactive paddlers report osteoarthritis or carpal tunnel in their fingers and wrists, tendonitis in their elbows, and the dreaded rotator cuff tear.

Take precautions to prevent these by using proper paddling techniques and taking care of yourself after a long day of paddling.

Fractures

- If pain persists, if there is deformity or difficulty moving the limb, treat as a fracture and summon help to get to a hospital.

- If you are out on the water and help cannot reach you, do your best to immobilize the limb.

- Use a sling to immobilize a broken arm, a splint on a broken leg. You can also bandage a broken leg to the sound one.

- Protect protruding bone with dressing.

Shoulder Dislocation

- This injury can happen in whitewater paddling or sea kayaking in surf conditions.

- Do not try to reposition a dislocated bone into its socket.

- Immobilize the limb to reduce pain and get to a hospital.

- Strapping a PFD around the torso and arm is a good way to stabilize the limb.

- A kayaker who dislocates her shoulder will need to be transported with a contact tow (see page 132).

HYPOTHERMIA & HEAT ILLNESS
Know how to prevent and treat illness due to extreme temperatures

Here we'll discuss how to prevent and identify the early signs of these maladies as well as what initial treatment to give until you can get medical attention.

Minor cases of numb fingers, mild dehydration, and border-line hypothermia may not require a trip to the emergency room. But knowing when to take that step is vital.

Cold shock from sudden immersion in cold water happens immediately. Hypothermia is more gradual. After a wet rescue, be on the lookout for developing signs of hypothermia, even if the air temp is warm.

If the person cannot speak or loses consciousness, that's a no-brainer: Get help immediately. But even mild cases can get worse quickly, so if your treatment doesn't have an effect quickly, get professional help.

Preventing Hypothermia and Frostbite

A warm hat is the best way to prevent heat loss.

- Dress in layers and paddling gear appropriate to the water temperature and weather forecast (see Chapter 3).

- Have appropriate layers for wind, rain, and cold for everyone in the group and encourage their use.

- Nibble high-energy foods and stay hydrated. Bring a Thermos of hot tea if paddling in cold weather.

- Pay special attention to children whose small bodies and higher metabolisms are more sensitive to extremes than those of adults.

Treating Hypothermia

- Warning signs: uncontrollable shivering, clumsiness, slurred speech, weakening pulse for hypothermia; numbness or prickling pain for frostbite.

- Get off the water and seek a warm, dry shelter.

- Remove damp clothing and add layers of dry clothing. Give warm drinks (no alcohol) and high-energy snacks.

- Seek medical help immediately if the person is unconscious or if the condition does not improve.

If the person has an existing condition like diabetes or heart or kidney disease or is extremely young or elderly, play it safe and get medical attention.

It's never a bad idea to take a first aid course. A course in wilderness first aid is even better because basic first aid teaches you simply to stabilize a victim until help arrives. On the water, that could be hours away.

ZOOM

Treating frostbite: If possible, go to a warm, dry shelter. Remove wet clothing. Use body heat to warm the affected area: Put hands under the armpits, behind the knees, or on the stomach. Do not rub because doing this can damage skin. If feeling does not return soon, or if the tissue is blue or black, seek medical help to prevent permanent damage or loss of tissue.

FIRST AID

Preventing Heat Illness

- Stay hydrated by taking frequent water breaks, especially in humid weather, but also in cold weather, which depresses the body's natural thirst mechanism.

- If you feel overheated, dip a bandanna in a stream and put it around your head or dip your shirt and let it dry on your back.

- Keep a close eye on the kids: Children overheat more easily than adults.

- Wear a sunhat, sunglasses, and light-colored, long-sleeved shirt.

Treating Heat Illness

- Symptoms: nausea, headache, dizziness, confusion, cramps, lack of urine, damp, pale skin, fast pulse.

- Give fluids. Cool the person down by having him rest in the shade. Place a wet towel or bandanna on the face and neck.

- Monitor body temperature and symptoms. If they do not subside, get help.

- Dehydration and heat exhaustion can lead to life-threatening heatstroke.

157

EMERGENCIES
Know when to call for help and have an emergency plan

Certain situations require immediate medical intervention. Others can wait until you drive to an emergency room or doctor's office or even until you get home and see your own doctor.

Assess the situation clearly but not rashly and do not panic.

Clearly if a person is not breathing, has no pulse, is bleeding severely, has a protruding bone, or is unconscious, you should call for help right away.

Shock is a potentially life-threatening condition that can sneak up on you. Shock is a failure of the circulatory system that can be caused by severe blood loss, severe burns, fractures, heatstroke or hypothermia, or lightning strike.

Even people with a seemingly mild injury can slip into shock, so it's important to monitor them, know the signs, and

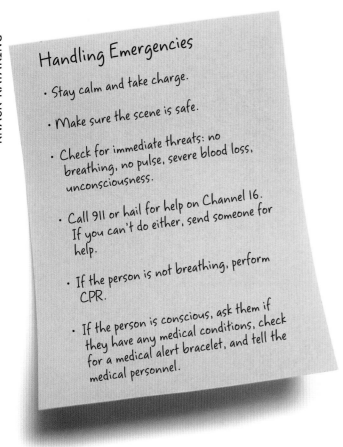

Handling Emergencies

- Stay calm and take charge.

- Make sure the scene is safe.

- Check for immediate threats: no breathing, no pulse, severe blood loss, unconsciousness.

- Call 911 or hail for help on Channel 16. If you can't do either, send someone for help.

- If the person is not breathing, perform CPR.

- If the person is conscious, ask them if they have any medical conditions, check for a medical alert bracelet, and tell the medical personnel.

Shock

Take a pulse with two fingers on the inner wrist, just below the thumb.

- Shock can be caused by severe blood loss, severe burns, fractures, lightning strike, heatstroke, or hypothermia.

- Symptoms: fast, weak pulse; cool, pale skin; chills; confusion; lack of urine.

- Action: Until help arrives, keep the person warm, calm, and comfortable, lying down, with legs elevated. Do not give food or drink.

- Monitor breathing and pulse rate, taking notes to give emergency personnel.

get professional medical help immediately.

Use a cell phone to call 911 or a marine radio to hail for help on Channel 16. If neither is possible, send someone to get help and stay with the victim. If help cannot get to you, tow the victim in his or her kayak, doing a contact tow if possible (see page 132).

(see page 132).

YELLOW ● LIGHT

If you hope for the best and plan for the worst, you could save someone's life. Always have a bail-out plan on the water in case extreme weather comes up, or someone is ill or injured. Have a chart and/or a GPS unit so you can tell rescuers your exact location.

Rescue Breathing

- Take a Red Cross CPR course for training in this technique.

- If a person is unconscious but breathing, attempt to revive them while assessing the cause.

- If the person is not breathing, clear the airway and start rescue breathing.

- Use a plastic face shield to prevent the spread of germs.

CPR

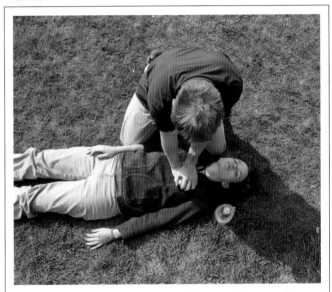

- Take a Red Cross CPR course for training.

- This technique has changed recently, so if it's been a few years, retake the course.

- If a person has no pulse and is not breathing, do a combination of rescue breathing and CPR chest compressions.

- Continue until medical help arrives.

TOOLS FOR NAVIGATION
Don't leave home without them

Like the carpenter and her tools or the artist and his pallet, every kayaker should head out onto the water properly equipped. When it comes to navigation, tops among the gear are a nautical chart or topographic map and a compass. A GPS unit is handy, as is a pair of binoculars (hint: binoculars are not just for birdwatching!).

Charts come in all manner of size, scale, and detail. Whatever shape or form, they are all based on a series of nautical charts produced by the National Oceanic and Atmospheric Administration's Office of Coast Survey. Established by Thomas Jefferson in the nineteenth century, this agency has charted and kept updated some 3.4 million square nautical miles of coast, seas, and inland waterways.

Having a chart doesn't necessarily mean you know where

Your Road Map on the Water

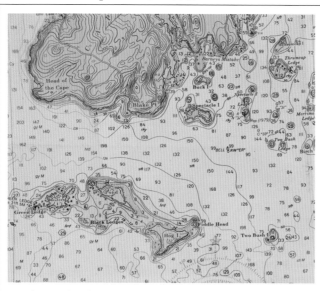

- Relevant details on nautical charts for kayakers include water depth (also called "soundings"), shoreline features, topographical features, aids to navigation like buoys and beacons, and hazards and cautions about bridge heights, submerged pipes, or wrecks.

- Large-scale charts contain in-depth details about a small area. They're useful for near-shore navigation.

- Small-scale charts cover a large area and lack the near-shore details. These are good for long-distance, open-water navigation.

A Kayaker-friendly Navigation Tool

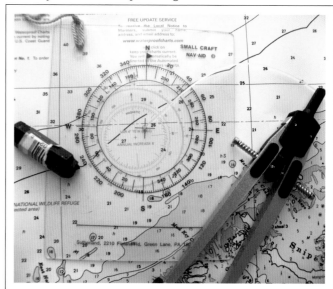

- The Small Craft Nav-Aid is a navigating tool designed by Chuck Sutherland.

- It is a lightweight, clear plastic rectangle (4 by 5 inches) imprinted with a compass rose. A plastic string, called a "bearing line," is attached at the center of the compass rose.

- Sutherland has written a booklet that comes with the Nav-Aid that describes how to use his tool.

- With a waterproof marker and a chart, a kayaker can use this aid to take bearings for long open-water crossings or determine proper direction in poor conditions.

you are. Every chart features a compass rose, and every kayaker should carry a compass in their "what if" bag. It should go without saying: Knowing how to use a compass to pinpoint your location and plot a course helps, too.

Perhaps no other tool has revolutionized travel on land or water as much as the GPS unit. You can enter longitude and latitude coordinates for a location, hit your navigation feature, and the unit points the way. You can set the GPS unit to record your route as you paddle. If it's nightfall, or if a fog has set, you can trace the trail back to your put-in.

Be forewarned: GPS units are electronic and subject to battery failure or corrosion or ruin in water environments. That's why we champion them as a secondary form of navigation, not as a replacement for basic chart reading and compass skills.

Save the Location of Favorite Spots

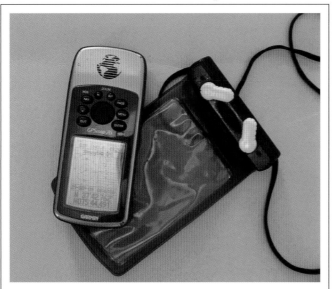

- A GPS unit uses satellites in space to pinpoint your location on Earth.

- With a GPS unit, your location is translated into latitude and longitude coordinates. With practice, you can plot your GPS location on a nautical chart.

- You can also load a GPS unit with preselected waypoints. The unit's navigation feature will help guide you from one point to another.

- Use a GPS unit to find your favorite fishing or swimming hole or a critical creek entrance.

Bring the Distance into Focus

- With high-powered waterproof binoculars you can read far-off buoys and markers or search for a place to land.

- Pick a style that has durable rubber casing to withstand water and salt corrosion.

- Binoculars for navigation should feature a magnification of 7 or greater and an objective lens size of 50 or greater.

- Beware of binoculars that claim to be "water-resistant" or "splashproof." These traits are not the same as waterproof.

RULES OF THE "ROAD"
Be a responsible mariner and paddle safely

When paddling with new kayakers in an area of heavy boat traffic, I catch their attention by repeating the folly that the only vessels a kayak need give way to on the water are a sailboat and a seaplane.

We follow this statement immediately with more sound advice. On the water in a kayak, we operate by the rule of tonnage: If an oncoming vessel is bigger and heavier than you, get out of the way and use extreme caution!

"Why bother learning the rules of the road?" you may ask. Your favorite kayak route is close to shore, and you avoid boat channels and the resulting game of chicken with oncoming powerboats.

The answer is simple. A kayaker is a mariner, and it is the mariner's responsibility to learn how to navigate with other

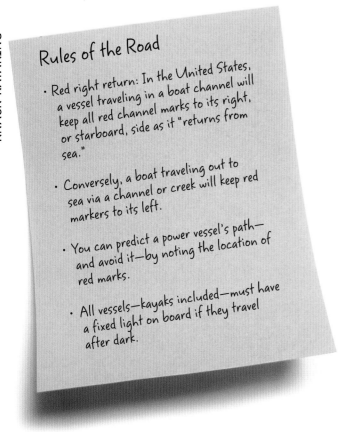

Rules of the Road

- Red right return: In the United States, a vessel traveling in a boat channel will keep all red channel marks to its right, or starboard, side as it "returns from sea."

- Conversely, a boat traveling out to sea via a channel or creek will keep red markers to its left.

- You can predict a power vessel's path—and avoid it—by noting the location of red marks.

- All vessels—kayaks included—must have a fixed light on board if they travel after dark.

Channels Are Best Avoided

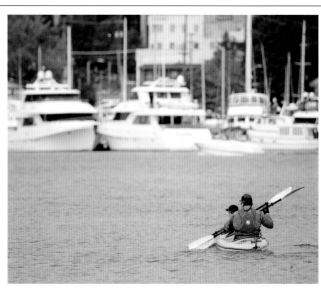

- A boating channel is a passage with deep water and is a safe, predictable route of travel for deep-draft vessels such as motor boats.

- Official boat channels are marked by green square and red triangle channel markers. They may have numbers or number/letter

combinations for identification. Some markers may be lighted; others are not.

- Local residents may maintain unofficial channel markers. Popular materials are white PVC pipe, bamboo sticks, or willow branches.

boats on water. This means learning and interpreting the nautical road signs. It might be a buoy, a lighted beacon, a day beacon (not lighted), or a day marker. Whatever shape or form, they are handrails that mariners use to navigate safely into harbors, through channels, and out to sea.

At the risk of being archaic, we recommend at some point reading Nathaniel Bowditch's *The American Practical Navigator*. It is an encyclopedic reference book to all things related to piloting your boat. Although much of it pertains to cruising and ocean-faring vessels, it provides all mariners with the necessary background and technical description of navigational aids and how they've developed.

As you learn the fine points of navigation, we have a few short-cuts that will help you get from Point A to Point B safely.

Look Both Ways Before Crossing

- Crossing channels can be done safely with prior planning and an understanding of what risks lie ahead.

- Approach a channel carefully. Look in both directions for powerboat traffic. Take time to gauge an approaching boat's direction of travel and approximate speed.

- When crossing, make a beeline for the other side of the channel. Don't dawdle in the middle or take a long, angular crossing line.

- When paddling in a large group, cross a channel as a single pod of kayaks rather than single file or spread out.

Heighten Your Visibility

- In a busy boat channel or harbor, kayaks are easy to miss.

- A sailing or power boater's attention is usually on safely navigating through crossroads and around other boats.

- Use a paddle that has a brightly colored blade to attract attention if needed. Increase your visibility at night by adding reflective tape to the front and back of your paddle blade.

NAUTICAL MARKERS
Beacons and buoys help you steer the right course

On land, to help navigate safely, you use traffic lights and stop, yield, and speed limit signs when driving.

Boaters use a corresponding system of signs for safe navigation. These navigational aids are plotted on nautical charts. With study and careful reconnaissance, kayakers can visually locate a navigation aid and find their corresponding position on a chart.

Broadly speaking, navigation aids on the water are categorized as beacons and buoys. A fixed beacon may be a simple post with a square or triangle with a number pasted on it. A floating buoy may have lights that flash in a sequential order, or it may have bells, gongs, or whistles. These aids may be bicolored: the upper half red and the lower half green or half red and half white. Or they may be yellow, which is a warning

Road Signs on the Water

- A channel marker helps define a channel or passage.

- A red channel marker is triangular and displays an even number identification.

- A green channel marker is square and displays an odd number identification.

- Remember this rule of all mariners: red right return. A boat returning to port in the United States will always keep the red marks to the right, or starboard, side of the boat.

Reaching an Intersection

- If you must cross through an intersection, look carefully to the channel markers to help predict other boats' routes of travel.

- If a single marker features red on the top and green on the bottom, the color on top is the controlling color

 for boat traffic returning from sea to port.

- If a single channel marker post has both a green square and a red triangle, and they face opposite directions, these are road signs for boats entering and leaving the inlet or harbor.

of a hazard area such as a shoal or wreck.

Every nautical marker carries a message. It is up to us as mariners to learn what each marker tells us. They also serve as an "I am here" mark; if you see a green "Channel Marker 29" en route, you can find its location on your chart and estimate how much farther it is to the boat ramp.

Don't restrict yourself to on-water markers. More than once I've used a cell phone tower or radio tower to help orient my boat in the right direction.

ZOOM

The website www.uscgboating.org holds a trove of information on safe boating. Coast Guard auxiliary units will often hold safe boating courses in the spring and fall. Although not mandatory for kayakers, taking a safe boating course will help teach you basics on safe navigation on the water. The Coast Guard also enforces various boating rules, such as lighting requirements for kayaks traveling at night.

Floating Nav Aids

- A buoy is a navigational aid used in situations where a beacon would be impractical. A navigational buoy's position is fixed to the sea bottom by a mooring.

- Buoys may also mark hazard areas, such as a shoal.

- Like beacons, buoys feature distinct colors, shapes, top marks, numbers, and lights. These marks dictate its function, whether to help you avoid a hazard or to steer you to safe water.

- Buoys also may have a sound feature, like a gong, whistle, horn, or bell.

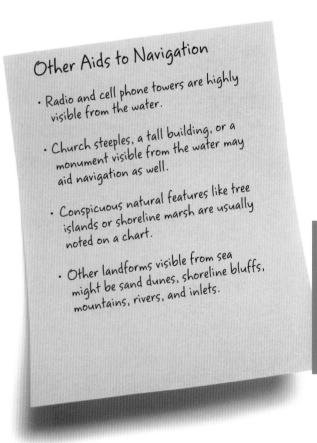

Other Aids to Navigation

- Radio and cell phone towers are highly visible from the water.

- Church steeples, a tall building, or a monument visible from the water may aid navigation as well.

- Conspicuous natural features like tree islands or shoreline marsh are usually noted on a chart.

- Other landforms visible from sea might be sand dunes, shoreline bluffs, mountains, rivers, and inlets.

NAVIGATION

CHART READING
Learn this skill before heading out onto the water

At first glance, a nautical chart can seem an intimidating document. It is filled with all sorts of strange symbols, incoherent abbreviations, a variety of colors, and small numbers everywhere. Believe it or not, all of it really does mean something.

Nautical charts are our road maps on the water. At their most basic, they reproduce an area of the Earth on paper. The official government charts, produced by the National Oceanic and Atmospheric Administration's Office of Coast Survey, cover U.S. coastal regions, harbors, and navigable inland waters like the Chesapeake Bay, Puget Sound, and the Great Lakes.

Because official charts are meant to provide accurate, up-to-date information for marine trade, their size and scale may exceed what most kayakers need.

An Important Reference Book

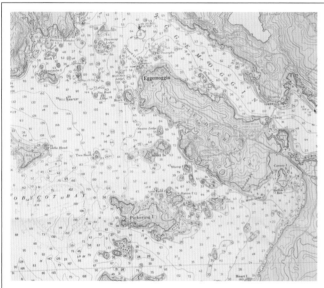

- Chart No. 1 lists and describes all features found on NOAA charts.

- Copies of Chart No. 1 can be downloaded free at www.nauticalcharts.noaa.gov/.

- This book is designed for cross-referencing. If you see a symbol or abbreviation and don't recognize it, you can find its explanation in Chart No. 1.

- Chart No. 1 is not practical for use in a kayak. Instead, you should study it before you head out onto the water.

Which Way Is Up? North, of Course.

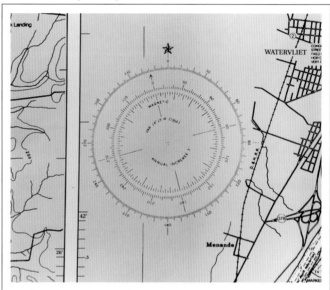

- All charts, whether official NOAA charts or commercial variations, feature a compass rose.

- The rose is a circle featuring the four cardinal directions—north, south, east, and west—as well as degrees marked from 0 to 360.

- Compass roses feature both true north and magnetic north. The difference between the two is called "variation."

- The Small Craft Nav-Aid is ingeniously designed to be used with a chart's compass rose to help you plot a course of travel.

Or you may find that you kayak in an area not covered by nautical charts. Inland lakes in the Adirondacks of New York or the many lakes and rivers in Maine offer wonderful paddling experiences, but you won't find them on any chart.

In these cases, kayakers can find useful substitutes by using United States Geological Survey (USGS) topographical maps or high-quality, up-to-date satellite or aerial imagery of wherever they paddle.

Because official NOAA charts are so unwieldy, many of us use commercial versions of them. Mapmakers such as DeLorme, MapTech, Waterproof Charts, or Top Spot splice NOAA maps together to cover a well-traveled area. Or they use just part of a NOAA chart and enlarge the scale to provide better detail.

Whichever form of map or chart you use, it's important to study it before you go out onto the water. Forewarned is forearmed.

Symbols and Abbreviations

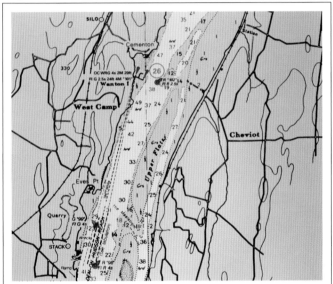

- Charts display natural features such as shorelines or rocky bluffs, cultural features such as buildings and memorials, and lights, buoys, and beacons.

- Water depths, or soundings, are labeled on charts as well. Be sure to check if soundings are measured in feet or fathoms.

- Channel markers, lights, and buoys are represented in the same color as they appear in the field.

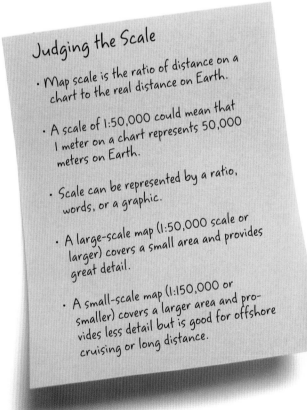

Judging the Scale

- Map scale is the ratio of distance on a chart to the real distance on Earth.

- A scale of 1:50,000 could mean that 1 meter on a chart represents 50,000 meters on Earth.

- Scale can be represented by a ratio, words, or a graphic.

- A large-scale map (1:50,000 scale or larger) covers a small area and provides great detail.

- A small-scale map (1:150,000 or smaller) covers a larger area and provides less detail but is good for offshore cruising or long distance.

COMPASS & NAV-AID
Keep it simple and ignore the bells and whistles

Some compasses are simple round ornaments with a magnetic needle (the perennial stocking stuffer that may or may not feature a key ring!). Some have a flip-up mirror. Another style slides out of a case. There are digital compasses and magnetic compasses that don't feature needles at all. Some have luminous numbers for easy reading at night. Others feature a small magnifying glass for close examination of map or chart features.

This is one area where staying simple is best. Ignore the bells and whistles. If you don't know how to use a compass, they amount to little. Stick to simple, learn the skill, then accessorize as you deem necessary.

By "simple" we mean one of two devices: the orienteering compass and the Small Craft Nav-Aid. They're not mutually exclusive. A safety-minded kayaker carries both.

Take a Bearing

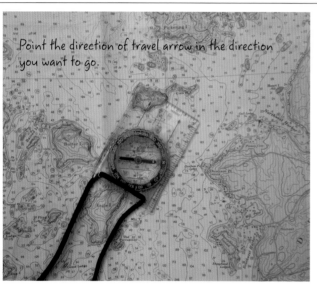

Point the direction of travel arrow in the direction you want to go.

- Hold the compass flat out in front of you, close enough that you can still read the magnetic needle and numbers.

- Turn your body until you point toward your destination. Grip the base plate so it won't move, and rotate the compass housing.

- Rotate the housing until the "North" mark (usually a bright red arrow imprinted on the base plate) matches up with the magnetic needle.

- Note the degree that matches up with your direction of travel arrow. That is your bearing.

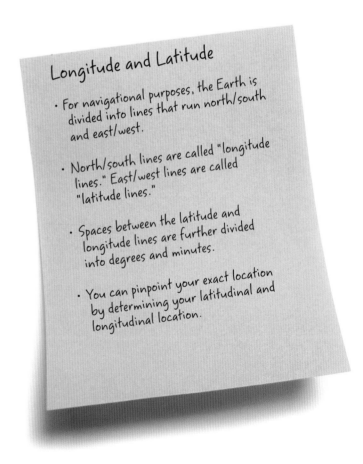

Longitude and Latitude

- For navigational purposes, the Earth is divided into lines that run north/south and east/west.

- North/south lines are called "longitude lines." East/west lines are called "latitude lines."

- Spaces between the latitude and longitude lines are further divided into degrees and minutes.

- You can pinpoint your exact location by determining your latitudinal and longitudinal location.

The orienteering compass features a round housing that holds a magnetic needle. It's set upon a clear plastic base plate. A "direction of travel" arrow is etched on the base plate. Within the round needle housing is a "North" mark that comes in quite handy, as we shall see.

The Small Craft Nav-Aid takes simplicity to the next level. It is a square piece of plastic imprinted with a compass rose, with a piece of synthetic line attached to the center. With planning, this and a waterproof marker are all you'll need for on-the-go navigation.

Nav-Aid

- Setup of the Nav-Aid requires a waterproof marker, straight edge, and a nautical chart.

- First, plot the Nav-Aid against your chart's compass rose.

- Next, draw true north on the Nav-Aid with a permanent marker and straight edge. Do the same for the nearest east/west latitude.

- You can establish a bearing from any location by placing the center of the Nav-Aid on your known location and stretching the Nav-Aid's synthetic bearing line toward your known next stop.

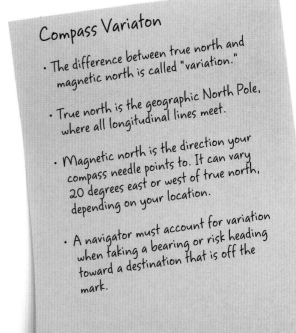

Compass Variaton

- The difference between true north and magnetic north is called "variation."

- True north is the geographic North Pole, where all longitudinal lines meet.

- Magnetic north is the direction your compass needle points to. It can vary 20 degrees east or west of true north, depending on your location.

- A navigator must account for variation when taking a bearing or risk heading toward a destination that is off the mark.

ON-WATER NAVIGATION
Planning is the key to on-water navigation

Seated in a kayak, bobbing offshore, you take stock of what's before you. Perhaps you're on a beautiful lake fringed with pine trees. Or gliding between mangrove islands. Maybe you're approaching a busy channel with lights blinking at random.

You may be set to cross a 2-mile-wide creek but cannot pinpoint any prominent land features on the other side. Or you're facing a cliff, a headland, or a city skyline.

You reference your chart, set a compass bearing, and have key points as backup in your GPS unit. You can distinguish between the various flashing lights, and you know there are also some day beacons that will serve as handrails.

On-water navigation is a combination of both planning and experience. If you happen to have no experience in an area you're kayaking, you can be comforted by using chart-

Set Up for Success

- Arrange your navigation tools on the kayak for fast, easy referencing.

- Slip the chart under deck bungees forward of the cockpit. Have the chart arranged to show the area where you're traveling.

- Turn on the GPS unit, which should be set inside a clear drybag. We attach ours to the forward deck bungees.

- Have your orienteering compass handy, either stuffed in a PFD pocket, in a close-by drybag, or hanging around your neck.

Check Out Your Surroundings

- Make a visual inspection of your surroundings and mark your location both on your chart and with the GPS unit.

- Look for prominent landmarks, either natural or human-made. Radio towers, power lines, monuments, or tall buildings can become

- navigational aids.

- With your location established, look ahead to where you want to go.

- Look for handrails such as channel markers, lights, or buoys that can help guide you to your destination.

reading skills, knowing how to use a compass, and establishing landmarks as reference points.

We refer to such landmarks as "handrails." Think of it like this: People walking downstairs in the dark will hold a handrail as they descend. So, too, when navigating, you can use landforms, beacons, or buoys as constant guides and references as you travel.

Natural Ranges and Drift

- A natural range is any two objects on your line of travel. It could be a channel marker and distant island or a house and a cell phone tower behind it.

- Align the objects one behind the other and steer a course toward them.

- If wind or current is causing your kayak to drift, your range will become misaligned.

- Compensate for drift by adjusting your course right or left until your natural range comes back into alignment.

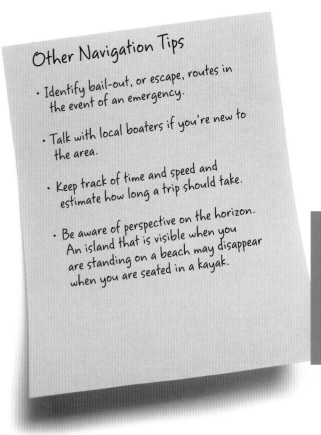

Other Navigation Tips

- Identify bail-out, or escape, routes in the event of an emergency.

- Talk with local boaters if you're new to the area.

- Keep track of time and speed and estimate how long a trip should take.

- Be aware of perspective on the horizon. An island that is visible when you are standing on a beach may disappear when you are seated in a kayak.

DANGEROUS WEATHER
Hope for the best, plan for the worst

The best way to handle dangerous weather is to avoid it. Check up-to-date weather reports and radar online before heading out. While on the water, listen to NOAA Weather Radio on your handheld marine radio.

Despite the forecast, we are well aware of how a summer thunderstorm can materialize in minutes.

If you are in summer thunderstorm season, paddle early in the day because thunderstorms tend to develop in the afternoon. You do not want to be on the water during a thunderstorm.

Keep an eye on the clouds as well. White puffy clouds are called "cumulus clouds." If they're isolated and small, they're an indicator of fair weather. However, if cumulus clouds start piling up into towering balls, that is a sign that severe

Flooding

- Flooding can change the shape and course of a river.

- River levels will rise after a heavy rain. Obstructions that can be fatal to kayakers, such as a downed tree, may be hidden by high water.

- On a camping trip, a simple way to measure the water's rise and fall over time is with a stick at water's edge.

- Whitewater paddlers can check levels on their favorite rivers at www.american whitewater.com.

Lightning

Sit on a mattress pad if available to insulate you from the ground.

- At the first sound of thunder, get off the water immediately.

- If you can't reach shelter, find a grove of trees of roughly the same height (avoid standing under a solitary tree or the tallest tree around).

- If there are no trees, find a ravine or other low spot.

- Squat down as low as possible, balancing on the balls of your feet. If you cannot hold this position, sit with your knees drawn up.

weather is approaching.

A sudden change in temperature for the cooler is another sign of summertime thunderstorms. By the time you feel the cool gusts, time is short before severe weather arrives.

Take the risk of lightning seriously. Approximately seventy Americans are killed each year by lightning strike, and hundreds are injured. The good news is that lightning strikes can be avoided with a few simple precautions.

If you see the telltale funnel of a tornado or a spit of dark cloud dangling from a larger one, take shelter immediately.

Fog

- Fog can move in on coastal waters quickly and without warning, making a small kayak extremely vulnerable to larger boats that cannot not see it.

- Wearing a headlamp will make you more visible if you get caught in fog, as will reflective tape on your boat, PFD, jacket, or paddle.

- If you travel where fog is common, consider adding a handheld foghorn to your safety equipment.

- Members of groups should stay close together and use their whistles if they get separated.

NOAA Weather Radio

- This nationwide network broadcasts continuous weather information, including wind speed and direction and the roughness of the water.

- Scan weatherband Channels 1 through 9 to find the one that comes in best in your immediate area.

- Listen for your location, usually described by land points and marine buoys (refer to your nautical chart).

- NWR will give you immediate weather and warnings as well as forecasts for the next week.

WAVES & SWELLS
Go with the flow

NOAA Weather Radio reports include the amount of chop on the water as well as the height of swells.

The chop may be described as "heavy," "light to moderate," "light," or "smooth." The reports will also distinguish between near-shore and offshore conditions, which can help you decide how far away from land you should go.

Swells of 1 to 2 feet are not a problem for most paddlers.

When the forecast gets above that height, you may want to reconsider your trip or route based on your abilities.

At some point, you may want to push your own personal limits as to how big of a sea you can handle. Try to do this with a more experienced paddler and only if you are confident you can roll or get back into your boat in rough conditions.

If you are surprised by rougher seas than you expected,

Swells

- Keep your hips loose as you allow your boat to ride the troughs and peaks.

- If swells are coming fast and close together, ride them at an angle rather than parallel or straight on.

- In confused seas, just keep paddling. You are most stable when your paddle is moving through the water.

- In really big swells, you may lose sight of fellow paddlers in the troughs. Stay together.

Boat Wakes

When a boat passes you, it creates a series of swells called a "wake."

- When at all possible, stay out of channels that mark the deeper water for larger vessels.

- Don't let the waves hit your boat broadside, or you may flip over.

- Instead, point the bow of your kayak into the wake at an angle.

- Ride the wake but keep paddling. You are most stable when the paddle is moving through the water.

keep paddling and don't panic! If you feel you are in trouble, use your voice or your whistle to alert your paddling partners to stay close.

Cresting waves and surf present a technical challenge but can also be a lot of fun if you know how to ride them.

If you plan on surfing, consider wearing a helmet, using a short sit-on-top kayak, and taking a lesson.

Riding the Surf

- Position your boat so that the wave approaches the back and side of your boat.

- As the wave lifts you up, paddle furiously to "catch" the wave and let it propel you forward.

- Remember: A paddle blade in the water makes you more stable than a blade out of the water, so keep paddling.

- The wave's effect on the boat is to turn it sideways. If this happens, a capsize usually follows. Use a forceful stern rudder to correct your course.

When Is It Too Rough to Paddle?

- Be realistic in balancing your skills with the conditions.

- If you're a beginner, a NOAA small-craft advisory may indicate that conditions are too rough.

- Avoid rough-weather paddling if you do not have the equipment or skills for wet exit, reentries, and rescues.

- If you can hear thunder, get off the water as quickly and safely as possible.

- If water temperatures are below 55°F, and you do not have cold-weather paddling gear, it's not safe to paddle.

WEATHER & WATER

TIDES & CURRENTS
These are the vertical and horizontal movements of the Earth's waters

It's important to learn the differences among tide, current, and tidal current, what causes each of them, and how they affect paddling conditions.

Tide is the daily vertical movement of water up and down that's caused by gravitational forces of the moon and sun. Tides are very predictable, so you can refer to printed tide charts for your area or look them up online. Some places have one tide cycle a day, others have two.

The height of the tide is measured in feet and varies day to day and region to region. Tide height can also be affected by wind or a full moon. A high tide may cover a beach or expose a sandbar. In a salt marsh, a small creek may empty entirely of water at low tide, making it impassable. In that same marsh, if high tide coincides with a new moon or full moon, the levels

Tides

- As you paddle coastal waters, it's helpful to know if the tide is coming in or going out and the times for high and low tides.

- Get a printed local tide chart or go to www.salt watertides.com for coastal waters of the continental United States.

- Low tide can expose hazards to navigation such as oyster beds, mud flats, and rocks and make shallow creeks impassable.

- Ebb is the fall of the tide or "going out." Flood is the rise of the tide, and slack is when the tide is reversing and there's no tidal current.

Current

- Current is the lateral movement of water. Rivers and ocean have currents.

- The flow of current over rocks is what causes whitewater conditions.

- The flow will quicken beneath bridges, in narrow channels, and between pilings.

- Be careful paddling after a heavy rain or during a scheduled dam release.

could be so high that you can paddle across the top of the salt marsh cordgrass.

Current is the lateral movement of water, such as the flowing of a river. Current may increase on a river after a heavy rain or after the release of a dam.

Tidal current is a current caused by the rise and fall of a tide. You won't feel this so much in open water. In a channel or narrow tidal creek, you will definitely know if you are going with or against the tide.

Tidal Current

The speed of tidal current is measured in knots and can affect your paddling.

- Current is also created by the ebb and flow (fall and rise) of the tide.

- Tidal current can work with you or against you, depending on your direction of travel.

- Use a tide chart to time your trip so the tide works to your advantage.

- Be aware that a strong tidal current can carry you away from your desired destination or toward a hazard.

Confused Seas

- When a strong current or tidal current passes under a bridge or around a large bridge piling, choppy conditions can result.

- The mouths of large inlets and narrow channels or wind against tide conditions can also create confused seas.

- Waves rebounding off bridge pilings, bulkheads, or even a steep shoreline will create confused seas and turbulence.

- If at all possible, stay a safe distance from objects that create rebound.

WIND

It can be an aid or a hindrance to paddling

It's harder to work against the wind than with it. Just ask Bob Seger, who memorialized the futile efforts of paddling against the wind! He was talking about paddling, wasn't he?

A paddler can adopt strategies for working with, rather than against, the wind.

Weather reports, including NOAA Weather Radio, will give you the current and predicted wind speed (either in knots or miles per hour) and direction. The direction is given as a compass point, such as southwest or north-northeast. But it is the direction the wind is coming from, not the direction it is going.

Typically, wind speeds of 5–10 knots are not going to affect you that much. When speeds get to 15–20 knots, you may want to alter your day's paddling to fully take advantage of the wind direction. You probably shouldn't be on the water

Beam Wind

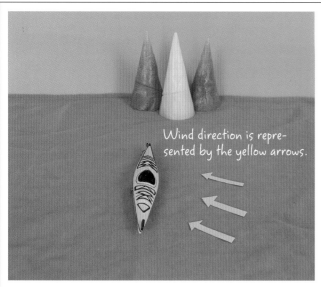

Wind direction is represented by the yellow arrows.

- When paddling toward a destination, a kayaker must take wind direction into account.

- A beam wind is one that comes at your kayak from the side.

- If you head toward your destination in a beam wind, the wind will push you off course.

- Kayakers should compensate for the wind pushing their kayak by adjusting course.

Ferrying

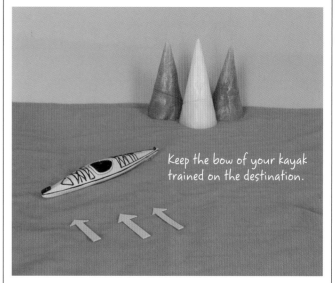

Keep the bow of your kayak trained on the destination.

- Ferrying is a method by which kayakers can compensate for the wind.

- If wind is coming from your right, pick a point that is slightly to the right of your destination.

- This maneuver is sometimes called "pointing up"

- the kayak. It helps compensate for the wind that is pushing you sideways.

- This kind of navigation requires constant adjustment so that you do not get blown past your destination.

at all in winds of more than 35–40 knots. These are called "gale force" winds.

Strong winds also cause choppy water, another challenge to consider. The Beaufort Wind Scale describes wind and water conditions to expect based on the wind speed.

With knowledge of wind direction and speed you can plan accordingly. You could paddle in the lee, or shelter, of the shoreline. Or you could forgo an open-water crossing into a headwind for a longer, round-about route that keeps you in the shelter of the land.

ZOOM

Synthesize three skill sets: reading nautical charts, understanding wind and weather, and understanding the effects of landforms. Put these together, and you'll have an effective bag of tricks to plan the perfect route. Keep in mind that wind forecasts can and do change through the day, so check often.

Attacking the Wind

- Add force to your forward stroke by "punching" the air with your upper hand as you rotate.

- A tailwind is not always a joy ride! It often requires frequent correction strokes, like a stern rudder, to keep the boat on course.

- Quarter oncoming waves by hitting them at an angle rather than head on.

- Use your skeg or rudder to help stay on a straight line of travel.

- Seek out the lee, or sheltered, areas for rest and regrouping.

The Lee

A lee is a calm area of water sheltered from the wind by land and trees.

- Use the topography of the shore to help shelter you from the wind.

- Because kayakers sit low, even low shrubbery or the edge of a salt marsh will block some wind.

- You can visibly see a lee because the water is calmer near shore than it is offshore.

- Even if you can't follow the shoreline the entire time, you can use the lee of islands to periodically rest from a strong headwind.

WEATHER & WATER

READING THE RIVER
Scout out hazards and a line of travel beforehand

When whitewater kayakers talk of reading the river, they are not referring to the canon of literature relating to river travel.

They are, however, searching for a story. It's a story told in the patterns of current and on the water surface. It's a story about where it's safe to paddle and what dangers lie in their way.

By scouting a river, kayakers can identify eddies, those valuable spots of calm water where they can rest and regroup.

They can identify dangerous holes and hydraulics. And they should be able to discern the safest line past strainers and other objects that threaten to pin them.

It's not all gloom and doom. A scout of the river may show there is a train of standing waves. Riding these can feel like you're on a roller-coaster. Playboaters seek out waves to surf.

Rivers change their story day to day, season to season. Don't

Eddy

Eddy

- An eddy is the area of calm water immediately downstream from an obstacle.

- In an eddy, water is actually flowing opposite the river current.

- Rocks create eddies, as do river bends, bridge pilings, outcrops, and other large, immovable objects.

- Whitewater kayakers use eddies as a place to rest and regroup.

Chutes

- Chutes are narrow stretches of river that flow between two objects, usually mid-river rocks.

- Because water is condensed into a smaller area, the current in a chute is faster than that of the river around it.

- Kayakers look for a V-pattern in the water as they approach a chute.

- A V-chute pointed downstream is a safe route to travel. Avoid a V-chute pointed upstream.

assume because you've run a stretch once that familiar features will be there forever. After heavy rains, a flood can change a quiet stream into a raging torrent. Small holes where you played become "keepers," holes that are big enough to trap you and your boat underwater should you capsize.

ZOOM

We describe here a few major river features, and for each one, there is usually a corresponding paddling skill. Catching an eddy and peeling out of an eddy help you take advantage of these important rest stops. Likewise, playboaters will surf and perform acrobatics in manageable holes. Ferrying can help you avoid a dangerous strainer. See Chapter 10 for descriptions of these paddling skills.

Holes

- Holes are created when the river flows over a submerged object.

- Rocks create holes, as do low-head dams.

- Large holes or steeply angled holes create a phenomenon called a "hydraulic."

- A hydraulic describes the recirculating nature of water in a hole.

- Accomplished playboaters will surf and perform acrobatics in a river hole. However, holes can pose a danger if you capsize and get sucked into the recirculating water.

Hazards on the River

- Floods can obscure river hazards like low-head dams and strainers.

- Low-head dams create holes that will pin you beneath the water.

- Strainers are any objects—most often fallen trees—that stop floating objects but let water through.

- Rushing water will pin you and the kayak against a downed tree and force you beneath the water.

WEATHER & WATER

CHILDREN
Make kayaking a family affair for all ages

The first question we are often asked by paddling families is, "How young is too young to go kayaking?"

We'd love to say there's no age limitation, but through experience we've found that most children under five or six simply don't sit still in a kayak for very long. Short trips close to shore are the way to ease children into paddling through positive experiences.

There are several ways to take young children paddling. They can sit in the front cockpit of a tandem kayak with an adult in the back. Some tandem kayaks come with a removable "jump seat" that fits between two adult paddlers. Very small children may be able to sit in your lap, but this is recommended only for short distances. They may not appreciate the water dripping off your paddle and onto their head!

A Child's Life Jacket

- Should be worn at all times, zipped and buckled up, no exceptions

- Should be Type III Coast Guard-approved and appropriate for the child's weight and size

- Should have a bright color and reflective tape

- Should have a crotch strap and a grab loop at the back of the neck for children under fifty pounds

In the Same Boat

Most parents will want to keep children in the same boat with them until age seven or so.

- Have the child sit in the front cockpit of a tandem or sit-on-top kayak with an adult in the back.

- For open-cockpit tandems, you can get a removable jump seat that fits between the two seats.

- Smaller children may be able to sit in your lap for short distances but only in a boat with a large cockpit.

- We don't recommend putting a child into an open hatch. Doing so greatly reduces the boat's flotation and your ability to empty the hatch of water after a capsize.

At a certain age and ability, usually not until seven or eight years old, children will be confident enough to paddle their own boat.

Children must always wear a life jacket when in any type of boat. It's Coast Guard regulations, and you can get a ticket for not obeying.

For safety and comfort, dress children in layers, according to the water temperature, not the air temperature (see Chapter 3).

ZOOM

Route planning: Be realistic, considering distance and conditions in relation to the youngest/weakest paddler in the group. Plan a route that has some rest stop options as well as a bail-out plan to shorten the trip if kids get antsy or there's an emergency.

Going Solo

- Parents can determine at what age, confidence level, and ability their children can start paddling solo.

- Children will have much more success with a boat and paddle suited to their smaller size.

- Be sure to attach a paddle leash so kids don't lose their paddle.

- Bring a tether or tow rope just in case of high wind or fatigue.

Whitewater for Kids

- Children should be about nine or ten years old before they start whitewater training. They should be confident swimmers.

- Be sure that children have the proper-size boat and helmet to fit them.

- Start practicing in a lake or calm water.

- We strongly recommend enrolling your children in a multiday clinic or camp to hone their skills.

ELDERLY
How old is too old?

We get asked quite a bit from older would-be kayakers: How old is too old? Our answer is "never!"

Kayaking hinges as much on attitude as age. The oldest people we've taken kayaking were a couple, eighty-two and eighty-three years old, respectively. It was the first time for both. They had so much fun that they didn't want the trip to end!

Most older people find getting into and out of the boat to be the hardest part. Once they're in, it's a breeze.

We recommend that you use wider, more stable boats for the first-time outing and go in calm, sheltered conditions not too far from shore.

Sit-on-top kayaks are easiest to get into and out of. They don't require lifting one's legs into a cockpit. You can float

Transportation Issues

Equipment that can help get your boat on the water:

- Roof rack systems tilt down to make car-top loading easier.

- A rear-loading rolling rack system takes some of the weight for you.

- A kayak cart makes it easy for one person to transport a boat to the water.

- If you are transporting a kayak to the water over sand, choose a cart that has big balloon tires.

Personal Assist

- Don't be afraid to ask for help getting into and out of your kayak.

- One person can straddle the bow or stern of the kayak, keeping it stable with his or her full weight.

- A second person can help the kayaker sit down in the boat and hand the kayaker the paddle.

- Whitewater boaters can get in on the bank and have someone push the boat into the water.

the kayak in calf-deep water and stabilize it while the person simply sits down on the boat (see next page for disabled paddlers).

Elderly kayakers should be realistic about their physical limitations. If you've paddled all your life, advancing age may not impact your routine as much as someone for whom kayaking is a lark or an occasional activity.

Whatever your abilities, you should consider what kind of shape you're in. And you should be aware you may have to deal with unforeseen events, such as a capsize.

Plan shorter trips with lots of scenic interest or wildlife. Bring your binoculars and bird book. The point is to get out on the water and enjoy yourself, not to go as far as you can.

Always let people you paddle with know of any serious medical conditions and bring vital medication in a drybag.

Take care of yourself and don't overdo it. Energy drinks or drinks with glucosamine for joint health can help. Afterward, ibuprofen and a hot bath will soothe aching joints and muscles.

Launching Devices

- The Yak-a-Launcher is a pontoon-type float that enables you to get into a kayak from a dock (www .getkayaktive.com).

- It makes a boat so stable that you can stand up in it.

- The unit disassembles easily so you can travel with it in your car.

- With a larger investment, you can purchase a floating kayak dock that allows you to slide off easily and paddle away (www.kayak dock.com).

Whitewater

- If you've never tried whitewater before, start easy with a course for beginners.

- Don't be discouraged if your first attempts at rolling are unsuccessful. It takes some flexibility and muscles you may not be accustomed to using.

- If you've been a whitewater cowboy for some time, just be aware of diminishing endurance and strength.

- There's no shame in going down a notch from Class IV to Class II or III rapids, and they can be just as much fun.

185

PADDLERS WITH DISABILITIES
Disability should not be a barrier to paddling

If you think about it, we are all challenged physically when it comes to traveling on the water. Without the assistance of a boat or kayak, none of us can float and glide across the water on our own.

Adventurers with disabilities often find that the sport of kayaking is a great equalizer. A properly fitted and adapted boat becomes an extension of the human body, allowing one to go unrestricted to places only dreamed of.

Even if the disability involves the arms, there are adaptive paddles, grips, and gloves that can help. Those people with sight, hearing, mental, or other physical impairments can all enjoy kayaking under the proper circumstances.

The beauty of kayaking is that it can be as strenuous or relaxing as you choose because there are so many environments,

Kayak for Two

- Just like with able-bodied beginners, often a wide, stable tandem kayak is a good way to start out.

- A person with an upper-body disability or injury can sit in the front and let the person in back do more of the paddling.

- The seat can be outfitted with foam pieces to keep the person secure.

- All paddlers should wear life jackets. Find one that fits and is easy to get on and off.

Solo

- Eventually you may want the freedom of paddling your own boat.

- Outriggers or sponsons can provide added stability.

- You should wear a spray skirt only if you have successfully practiced wet exits and reentries.

- You may still want to paddle with a buddy. Take a marine radio, flares, and other safety equipment.

from rugged whitewater to placid ponds.

Consider enrolling in a workshop or class specifically for disabled people. The American Canoe Association (ACA) offers two-day adaptive paddling workshops for people with disabilities and a four-day workshop for instructors and outfitters to teach them.

· · · · · · · · · · GREEN ● LIGHT · · · · · · · · · ·

If you can't find a workshop or class in your area, call your local outfitter to find out if it has anyone on staff who is trained in adaptive paddling. The ACA has a list of certified instructors (www.americancanoe.org), and you may be able to arrange private instruction.

Adaptive Paddles

- Special grips and gloves can be added to a regular paddle for those with arm disabilities or injuries.

- An adjustable cuff and grip will allow you to paddle with one arm.

- There's even a paddle that's operated with the legs on a sit-on-top kayak for those who have no use of their arms.

- Get the lightest paddle you can afford, made of carbon fiber or graphite to prevent unnecessary fatigue.

Seat Adaptations

- The standard seat in a kayak isn't designed to provide the support that a paraplegic or amputee will need.

- The cockpit of whitewater and sea kayaks can be outfitted with closed-cell foam to support the person's back and legs.

- A sit-on-top kayak can be fitted with a special seat for wheelchair users (www .disabledadventurers.com).

- Additional support can be obtained from a sturdy life jacket.

187

CONSIDERATIONS FOR WOMEN
Women can be just as good—even better—paddlers than men

Ladies, contrary to popular belief, don't necessarily need a lot of upper-arm strength or "big guns" to be proficient, even expert paddlers.

The secret is in the technique: rotating in sea kayaking and being able to read the water in whitewater kayaking.

By fully rotating during a well-executed forward stroke, you use the larger muscles throughout the torso. Paddling only with

your arms will tire you out much more quickly (see Chapter 8).

And because women are generally a bit more flexible than men, they can really perfect good rotation and form.

The independence you'll feel as you propel yourself through the water is extremely rewarding, and there's no reason you can't keep up with the guys.

Paddling has become increasingly popular with female

Paddle

Look for a small-shaft paddle, made for smaller hands.

- Buy the best (lightest) paddle you can afford, made of carbon fiber or graphite.

- Even if you get an inexpensive, plastic boat, don't skimp on the paddle. It will pay for itself in the long run in terms of endurance and the places you'll be able to go.

- Pay attention to length as well, getting the shortest possible for the width of your boat.

- Wear paddling gloves—three-quarter-length fingers in summer—to prevent blisters.

Women's PFD

- Don't settle for a "men's small" life vest.

- Many manufacturers are making PFDs specifically for a woman's frame.

- If you have large breasts, you will definitely want a style with cut-outs in the chest area.

- Get a vest with lots of compression straps to customize it to your frame.

- Always wear your lifejacket, buckled up and zipped, especially if you paddle alone.

paddlers, and thus a plethora of gear designed specifically for them has appeared on the market in recent years.

First and foremost, you need to find a boat that fits you. See Chapter 2 for getting a proper fit, paying particular attention to volume, or the amount of extra space in the cockpit.

Another important consideration is weight. Being able to lift your boat by yourself adds that much more independence. They are a larger investment, but lightweight materials like Kevlar allow you to get a high-performance sea kayak weighing in the forty-pound range.

ZOOM

Paddling while pregnant: Consult your doctor, of course, but many women find they can paddle even into their third trimester. Some things to consider:

- Morning sickness may be exacerbated by being on the water.
- As you get larger, you may feel more comfortable in a tandem.

Drop-seat

- If you often paddle in cold weather, a drysuit is a terrific option.

- But when nature calls, a drysuit is not easy to take off, especially if the weather is cold.

- Get a style with a zippered fly or drop-seat to make relieving yourself easier.

- Conversely, if you wear a wetsuit, it's OK to pee in it: It actually warms you up!

Answering Nature's Call

- Don't make the mistake of forgoing water intake to prevent having to urinate. Dehydration could result.

- When you can't get to a restroom, look for land where you can get out, or a shallow, hard-bottom area where you can get out and stand up to pee.

- If you are in deep water and absolutely cannot find a shallow place to get out, ask a close paddling buddy to pull alongside and steady your boat while you stand up in the cockpit to pee over the side. Balance is key!

- You can also purchase a handheld female urinal, basically a cup with a tube that goes over the side of the cockpit.

WARM-UP
Spend a few minutes stretching before and after you paddle

Recently people have debated the benefits of stretching before a strenuous workout. Basically, new research shows that stretching does nothing to prevent injury.

Speaking for ourselves and other paddlers we know, injury prevention isn't the main reason we stretch. We stretch to loosen up stiff muscles, increase flexibility, and just plain feel better after sitting in a boat all day.

As has been stated many times, rotation, rotation, and more rotation is the key to good paddling technique, from the forward stroke to rolling.

So anything that increases your flexibility is a good thing, whether it's traditional stretching, a yoga session, or even a massage. Men in particular seem to have tighter muscles and less flexibility in the hips and torso than women.

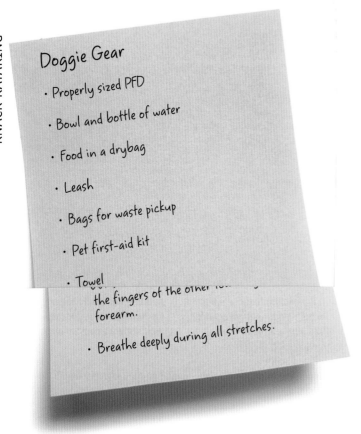

Doggie Gear

• Properly sized PFD

• Bowl and bottle of water

• Food in a drybag

• Leash

• Bags for waste pickup

• Pet first-aid kit

• Towel
the fingers of the other
forearm.

• Breathe deeply during all stretches.

Hamstring Stretch

- Do this stretch to keep your legs from getting stiff from sitting in the boat for long periods of time.

- You can do this on land or in the water (in calm conditions).

- Lean forward to hug the hull of your boat until you feel the stretch in your lower back and down your hamstrings.

- Hold for several seconds, take a deep breathe, release, and repeat a couple of times.

By alternately stretching and relaxing certain large muscles, you may feel more flexible almost immediately. If you do this as a habit over time, you'll find that these stretches can only add to your paddling repertoire and skill.

Oh, and just as in the forward stroke itself, don't forget to breathe!

Torso Rotation

- The purpose of this stretch is to loosen up the torso and hips for proper rotation

- Sitting in your boat, hold your paddle out in front of you, arms straight.

- Rotate to one side so that the paddle is parallel to the boat.

- You can drop the front blade down to use as leverage against the side of the boat.

- Hold for several seconds, perform on the other side, and repeat.

Shoulder Scrunch

- Purpose: to loosen up your neck and shoulders and reduce tightness

- Stow your paddle under a bungee and rest your hands in your lap, palms up.

- Shrug your shoulders up to your ears and hold for a few seconds.

- Release your shoulders, letting gravity and the weight of your arms let them sag. Repeat.

SKILL SESSIONS
Practice these skills so you'll be ready when you need them

It's one thing to intellectually know the steps to getting back into your boat after a spill. It's another to be able to do the steps in moving water or extreme conditions.

When the water is warm, we like to have Friday night skill sessions with our paddling friends. We kayak out to a beach, then start flipping over!

We coach and assist each other with various types of rescues, trying to add a new scenario into the mix each time. For instance, "Let's pretend I have a broken arm, and you have to get me back in my boat!"

There are many techniques and assistance devices for getting back into your boat. You'll find that some work better for you than others, depending on your boat, body type, and agility. Heavier people or those with very narrow boats will

Wet Exit and Reentry

Talk each other through the steps to reentry.

- Practice flipping and getting back in both with assistance and by yourself. (See Chapter 11 for detailed descriptions.)

- Practice using rescue equipment such as a paddle float, bilge pump, stirrup, and so forth.

- Keep adding new methods to your repertoire to keep things fresh.

- Next, graduate to practicing in rough water and high winds. These are the conditions under which you may get into trouble.

Backward Paddling

- Being able to gracefully paddle backward is useful in backing out of narrow creeks. It's also a fun way to show off your skills!

- Practice as a group by having paddlers line up in two parallel lines 5–10 feet apart.

- Take turns back paddling through the corridor formed by the two lines of paddlers.

- If you're practicing by yourself, paddle parallel to a bulkhead, a dock, or row of pilings.

find the cowboy entry almost impossible. You may also find that you prefer using a stirrup over a paddle float.

Practice will enable you to perfect the type of reentry that's best for you so you can perform it as quickly as possible in rough conditions.

Hip Flick

- This practice session is good for whitewater and sea kayakers to perfect their rolling.

- The person practicing should wear a spray skirt.

- Another person can stand in waist-deep water, with her palms extended to the paddler.

- The paddler can use these outstretched hands to practice edging and the hip flick.

Eddies

- Practice peeling in and out of eddies with a buddy.

- One paddler waits at the bottom of a rapid, giving directions and in a ready position for a rescue if needed.

- The practicing paddler can enter the "boiling water" to catch an eddy.

- When ready, practice "peeling out" of the eddy and returning to the waiting paddler for his or her turn.

195

AGILITY PRACTICES
Practice life-long learning

You know your basic strokes, you have a bag of tricks for self-rescue and rescue of others, and you may even be able to roll your kayak proficiently.

Congratulations! But now is not the time to let complacency keep you from learning new things.

There are always little tweaks you can do to perfect your forward stroke, turns, rolls, and edging. Learn from other paddlers, read or watch videos, and, of course, practice on the water.

In the winter, an indoor pool is a good place to practice with whitewater boats.

If you are really passionate about honing your paddling skills, consider taking the American Canoe Association's (ACA) Instructor Development Workshop (IDW) or a similar course

Edging

- Edging is a balancing skill that helps you maneuver and turn in both whitewater and sea kayaking conditions (see Chapter 9)

- You can practice edging by placing your hand on a dock for stability.

- When you're ready to try it unassisted, keep your paddle in the low brace position to recover if necessary.

- You can also have another paddler standing by in case you capsize and need a bow rescue (see page 124).

Draw Strokes

- Draw strokes are a fun and graceful way to turn sharply or move sideways through the water toward a dock or another boat.

- Practice by moving toward and away from a dock.

- Time yourself or race a partner to see who gets to the dock first.

- Practice different types of draws. A bow or stern draw will help you turn. A side draw or sculling draw will move your boat sideways.

196

offered by the British Canoe Union of North America (BCU).

Even if you never intend to teach, you will learn invaluable skills for your own personal paddling best.

Rolling is a skill that you lose if you don't use it. Practice it periodically so you'll be able to perform it when you need it.

ZOOM

Balance: Test the limits of yourself and your boat in calm, warm water. Wiggle your hips to see how far your boat can lean before going over. Climb up onto the rear deck of your boat. Capsize and right your boat, then try to paddle it full of water.

Playboating

Always wear a helmet and PFD and have a buddy paddle with you.

- Calm water is a good place to practice whitewater maneuvers.

- Do cartwheels, pirouettes, rolls, and other fun moves.

- When confident, proceed to moving water.

- If your roll isn't "bomb-proof," know how to do a wet exit and reentry and have a person standing by to do a bow rescue.

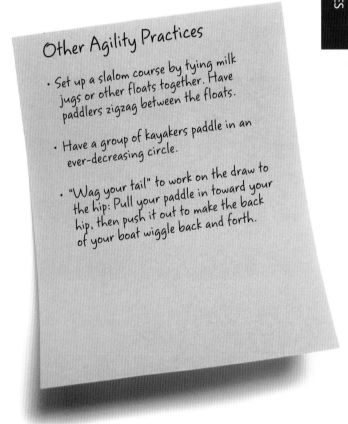

Other Agility Practices

- Set up a slalom course by tying milk jugs or other floats together. Have paddlers zigzag between the floats.

- Have a group of kayakers paddle in an ever-decreasing circle.

- "Wag your tail" to work on the draw to the hip: Pull your paddle in toward your hip, then push it out to make the back of your boat wiggle back and forth.

197

KAYAK GAMES

Games can help paddlers of all ages and skill levels

Playing games isn't just for kids! Lighten up a skills session with a little friendly, fun competition.

Of course, racing to a point like a dock, a tree, or shoreline is easy to do while on a kayak trip. Whitewater boaters can race to a point on the river below some rapids.

But there are other activities you can do as well to finesse your strokes, sweeps, rolling, and rescues.

Children are usually game for thinking outside the box—or boat, as it were! In warm water in a sheltered area, have all persons flip their boats, stand on their hulls, and try to paddle standing up (wider, plastic boats, of course). Then try various ways of getting back into the boats. Adults can practice sculling strokes by racing sideways toward a dock or counting how many strokes it takes to do a 360° turn.

Spin-off

Try to do the turn with as few sweeps as possible.

- Race another paddler to see how quickly you can perform a 360-degree turn.

- Have two kayaks facing each other. A third paddler yells, "Start."

- Use strong alternating forward and reverse sweeps

- to perform a complete turn so you end up facing each other again.

- You can do this on your own by counting how many sweep strokes it takes to complete the turn, then aiming to decrease the number each time.

Water Polo

- A group of four, six, or eight paddlers can form teams to play a game of water polo or soccer.

- You'll need two stationary objects, such as a dock, bulkhead, shoreline, pilings, or an anchored boat, to act as goals.

- Use your paddles to push a beach ball toward your goal, passing like you would in soccer.

- This game works best with shorter or whitewater boats that are more maneuverable.

Whitewater kayakers can practice making their rolls bomb-proof by doing several in succession.

Just be sure that you do your game-playing in controlled conditions and that no one goes too far beyond their comfort level. Have dry clothes and towels available and always wear life jackets and helmets (if whitewater kayaking).

ZOOM

Essential skills are reinforced through game-playing:
- Forward strokes and sweeps
- Balance
- Edging
- Flexibility
- Rotation
- Boat control

Conga Line

- Just like at a wedding, you can line up kayakers to play follow the leader!

- The person in front can serpentine, zigzagging to get everyone to practice sharp turns and edging.

- The conga line could also move from side to side using draw strokes.

- A whitewater conga line could have everyone do a roll one at a time down the line.

Other Games

- Relay races: Pass a bilge pump or other object down a line of kayakers.

- King of the mountain: Turn a kayak upside down and have one child try to stay on top.

- Sharks and minnows: In this variation on tag, a shark tags a minnow, who then becomes a shark and tags others. Eventually no minnows are left.

KAYAK FISHING
Get started in this fast-growing sport

If you already fish, transferring your skills and gear to a kayak is relatively easy. Even if you've never fished before, taking a rod along on your forays can be fun—and delicious!

Whether you catch dinner or practice catch-and-release, combining the two sports is a natural progression.

It's really taken off in recent years, with kayak manufacturers even designing boats just for the sport. The boats are typically wide and stable enough that you can even stand up to cast! Some have rod holders and bait wells.

The real beauty of kayak fishing is that you can get to places that most powerboaters cannot to find that secret fishing hole. Just practice discretion: Keep only what you can eat, release the rest, and follow local regulations for size and permits.

Casting

- You can use a spin reel or a fly rod.

- Practice first close to shore in case you lose your balance when casting.

- Some boats, particularly sit-on-tops, are stable enough to stand up in.

- Just be sure all your gear is waterproof and secure with tethers or bright-colored floats in case you take a spill.

Pedal Boats

- At least one manufacturer is making a boat with foot-operated pedals for hands-free paddling.

- Always have a paddle attached to your boat just in case you need it.

- The pedals lift out for launching or in case you encounter water that is too shallow to operate them.

- A lever on the side of the hull allows you to steer with one hand.

There's also the excitement of being so close to the water when you hook the big one for a really wild ride! Kayakers are even catching trophy-size fish from their boats.

Know what type of fish you might be after so you bring the right gear and bait or lures. Seek out some local knowledge from a bait shop or some anglers at a boat ramp.

If you are kayak camping, nothing tastes quite as good as fish you caught and cooked over a fire. Just be sure to bring a backup meal in case you don't get lucky!

Rod Holders

- Some boats come with rod holders, but you can also buy one and mount it on your own boat.

- They come designed specifically for either spin-cast or fly rods.

- A flush-mount rod holder can hold either type of rod.

- Consider the type that has a splash cover so it doesn't fill with water.

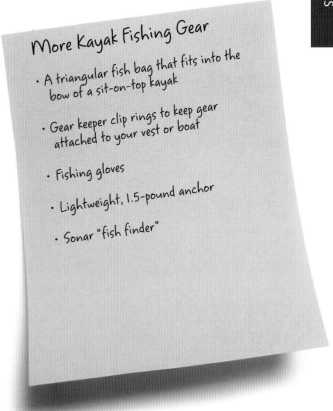

More Kayak Fishing Gear

- A triangular fish bag that fits into the bow of a sit-on-top kayak

- Gear keeper clip rings to keep gear attached to your vest or boat

- Fishing gloves

- Lightweight, 1.5-pound anchor

- Sonar "fish finder"

SNORKELING & DIVING
They are the ultimate kayak adventure

Combining snorkeling or diving with kayaking makes you both the captain and the engine of your own personal craft. It can take you where no tour boat can.

Just beneath the surface lie coral, sponges, sea life from starfish to sharks, and even shipwrecks.

Sit-on-top kayaks work best because they are stable enough to jump into and out of and to hold heavy dive gear on the deck. A snorkel and mask are easy items to throw into the hatch of any kayak.

There are a few things to consider, including stowing and securing the gear on the boat, getting beyond the surf zone safely (see Chapter 7), getting your gear on and off, and getting onto and off the kayak itself. A kayak diving specialty course is the fastest way to learn all you need to know.

Kayak Diving

- Sit-on-top kayaks made for diving come with a premolded tank well and straps to secure gear.

- Wear your boots and wetsuit (you can roll the top down if it's hot out). Preassemble the scuba unit so it's ready to go.

- Loading the boat: Center the weight and keep it low. Make sure everything is either in a hatch or tied down and tethered.

- Put your fins on first and take them off last. You can use them to propel yourself back on board.

Kayak Snorkeling

- All you need are snorkel, mask, and fins.

- Tether your boat to your ankle and pull it behind you as you explore.

- Always use a dive flag and wear your life jacket.

- Never touch sea life: You can damage fragile coral, or you may get stung!

What do you do with the kayak while you're in the water? If there are mooring balls or buoys, simply tie your boat to one. You can try a small anchor, but you cannot use it on coral or in deep water.

Tethering your boat to your ankle and pulling it behind you is a great solution for both snorkeling and diving (you may need a longer tether for diving). Make sure that hatches are closed and that your paddle is secure before going overboard.

Reentry

- Take off heavy gear and secure it in the kayak.

- Sit-on-top: Kick your fins to get your stomach on board, then swing your legs around to a seated position.

- Traditional sea kayak: Use a bilge pump and paddle float for reentry.

- Having another paddler stabilize your boat while you get back in makes it even easier.

Dive Flag

This red flag with a white diagonal stripe is available at most boating stores.

- If you don't have one, don't go! This piece of safety equipment is vital because it lets boaters see you.

- The red flag should be attached to a float or buoy and tethered to your boat or ankle.

- In most U.S. states you are required to use a dive flag and to stay within a certain number of feet of the flag.

- If you will be snorkeling farther from your boat, you can tether the flag to your ankle.

TRIP PLANNING
Who is going, where, and for how long?

In the beginning, no idea is too big or too small when deciding on an expedition. We turn to magazines, guidebooks, and narrative travelogues for inspiration.

As a favored destination emerges, that's when you start tailoring it to your skill level. Perhaps you dream of kayaking in Alaska. If you're a beginner, it may be a day-long guided tour that's part of a longer vacation itinerary. If you like exploring on your own, you may rent kayaks and spend a week exploring.

Choosing whom you travel with is oftentimes not given as much weight when planning a trip. Yet, day 2 of a ten-day trip is not the time to learn that a co-traveler has never launched in surf conditions. Or has chronic arthritic wrists.

It helps if all members in the group share the same goals.

Cool Weather Locales

- Camp on a pristine northern lake or the Maine coast, where your wake-up call is the cry of a loon.

- You will require seaworthy kayaks with bulkheads fore and aft and at least two hatches.

- In order to keep cold water out of your boat, you will likely be wearing spray skirts. This requires you to know how to do wet exits and reentries.

- Think "Safety First." Bring cold-weather paddling gear and do not wear cotton (see Chapter 3).

Southern Climes

- Paddle along a pristine wild beach or across Caribbean blue water.

- Pitch your tent right on the beach but follow local regulations and don't disturb nesting birds or sea turtles.

- Bring sun protection and drink plenty of water.

- Cold water temperatures is not an issue, as it is in northern climes, but you will have to cope with humidity, bugs, and the high hurricane season.

Achieving your destination is an obvious one, but don't overlook expectations about how many miles you'd like to travel each day or what constitutes an acceptable level of risk.

Kayak camping often means primitive camping. There may be no electricity or bathrooms, and you'll likely be quite far from civilization. (Then again, that's the beauty of it!)

Ease first-time campers and children into kayak camping by starting with a short paddle and a quick overnight.

ZOOM

Estimating daily distances: Sure, at a clip you can probably paddle your kayak 5 or 6 miles an hour. But could you keep that up all day? When you factor in fatigue, rest breaks, sightseeing, possible head winds, tides, or currents, you'll probably average 2 miles an hour over the course of a day. So for an expedition, 10–15 miles a day is a reasonable and comfortable goal for most paddlers.

Water Trails

Steps to Expedition Planning

- Research and choose a destination.

- Choose your party based on the principles of common interest and ability.

- Organize your equipment.

- Plan for weather, transportation, emergencies, and land support.

- Create a menu.

- Obtain necessary permits.

- Many states have water trails that show you where you can launch, camp, resupply, and even stop into a waterfront restaurant.

- Most trails have detailed maps and websites to provide you with trip-planning information.

- The entire coast of Florida is mapped in sections via the Florida Circumnavigation Saltwater Paddling Trail (http://floridapaddlingtrails.com).

- Another popular destination is the Maine Island Water Trail (www.mita.org).

CAMPING GEAR
Think minimalist when it comes to kayak camping

Before we ever kayaked, we were backpackers. The principles of compact, lightweight gear were drilled into our psyche.

Imagine our delight to learn how much you can fit into the hatches of a kayak.

True, if you are accustomed to car camping, with all that room available in the cargo area, you may have to downsize. In most cases, a large, bulky tent or a suitcase-style propane stove will take up too much room.

But that doesn't necessarily mean you have to make a huge investment. A small backpacking tent and single-burner stove are affordable. You could also rent from an outfitter who may also be able to rent you kayaks.

If you're planning on camping a lot, consider a stove that uses refillable liquid fuel bottles. You'll save money and you'll

Tent

Domed backpacking-style tents are compact and usually easy to set up.

- Even though you're camping light, sleeping comfortably is important.

- There are some items you simply can't improvise. A good tent is one. The right decision now will keep you warm and dry for many years to come.

- Remember that everything has to fit into your hatches, so consider a lightweight backpacking tent for two or three people.

- Dome tents are the most stable in high winds, free-standing, and usually have a good rain fly and vestibule.

Stove

A windscreen is necessary for optimal heating.

- Choose a single-burner stove with a refillable fuel container or a propane canister. Types of stoves and fuel include:

- Pressurized gas (propane or butane) in single-use canisters. Simply turn a knob and light the burner.

- Liquid fuel (white gas, alcohol, kerosene) bottles can be refilled. Fuel can be purchased by the half-gallon. They require priming and periodic cleaning.

- White gas and propane burn the hottest. Alcohol has very low heat output. Kerosene is smelly.

206

help save the environment. We've been using the same WhisperLite stove for more than ten years.

If you're just starting out and not ready to invest in all-new gear, borrow some from a camping friend or rent from an outdoor store. Look around the house or visit a thrift store for items you can repurpose for the outdoors. Check your kitchen cupboards for old or seldom-used cookware, mismatched utensils, or chipped coffee mugs that you can use to create your camping kitchen.

ZOOM

Wet set and dry set: When it comes to clothes, it's a good idea to separate them into categories. Your "dry set" stays dry always; in other words, you don't wear this clothing on the water. The "wet set" is your daily paddling clothes. You'll want to shed these when you get to camp, quickly if you're paddling in cold conditions.

Sleep Comfortably

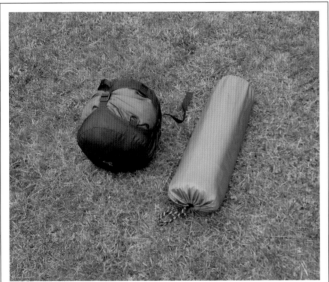

- Sleeping pads cushion but also protect you from ground cold and moisture.

- You can get inexpensive foam pads or pricier but more comfortable self-inflating mattresses.

- Sleeping bag choices include material (down versus synthetic), shape (mummy versus rectangular), and temperature rating.

- Inexpensive synthetic bags are fine for summer. Down bags are warmer and lighter but cost more and take a long time to dry.

EXPEDITION PLANNING

Basic Gear List

- Two- or three-person domed tent
- Sleeping bags and roll-up pads
- Single-burner stove
- Lightweight, nesting cookware
- Individual mess kits
- Clothes
- Food
- Light and extra batteries
- Personal toiletries, toilet paper
- Foldable, lay-flat chairs like Crazy Creek

KITCHEN GEAR
You can make easy or gourmet meals in the outdoors

Put some thought into what you will eat on your expedition for each day and each meal. That will determine what you'll need to store the food, keep it cold, and cook it.

Think like a backpacker would: lightweight and small. You'll need a single-burner stove that folds up, personal mess kits (including plate/bowl, mug/cup), cookware, utensils, dish soap, and sponge. Don't forget the matches or lighter and extra fuel for the stove.

A portable camp kitchen purchased from an outdoor store is very handy. It has all your cooking utensils and condiments organized in compartments in a zippered bag.

In meal planning, keep it simple. Think about items that won't spoil, that don't use a lot of fuel to cook, and that use just one pot.

Cookware

- Sets of nesting pots, like backpackers use, save space in your hatch.

- They usually come in three sizes, with foldable handles or a pot gripper if handle-less, and slip into a mesh ditty bag. Choose the size of your set based on the number of people.

- Choose lightweight cookware made of aluminum, stainless steel, or titanium.

- Flat lids with sides can be used as a plate or frying pan or flipped over on top of the pot to create a double boiler.

Lighting

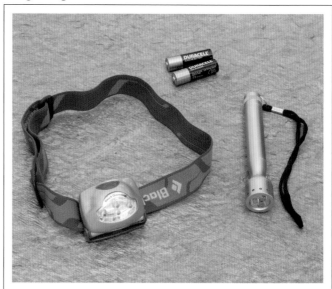

- A water-resistant headlamp with an adjustable elastic headband is an indispensable aid should you get caught out after dark on the water.

- A headlamp is hands-free so you can prepare a meal, set up a tent, or read in the dark.

- Don't forget spare batteries, preferably the rechargeable kind. Chargers can be solar-powered or plug into a car's cigarette lighter.

- A small battery-operated lantern or telescoping flashlight is good for general camp lighting.

208

As you get more experience cooking outdoors, you may become a gourmet! The key is being organized to be sure you have everything you need.

Water is extremely important. Find out whether you will have a fresh water source. If not, you'll have to bring all your water, roughly one gallon per person per day.

Drink only from known, potable water sources. There are three basic treatments for purifying water: boiling, iodine tablets, or a water filter/purifier.

ZOOM

Snacks should be sturdy and nonperishable:
- GORP, granola bars, fruit, crackers, pepperoni
- Breakfast: packets of instant oatmeal, hard-boiled eggs made at home, fruit, cereal bars
- Lunch: tuna or chicken wraps or pitas
- Dinner: dried backpacker meals; homemade meals frozen and allowed to thaw in the cooler; simple one-pot pasta or rice recipes

Water

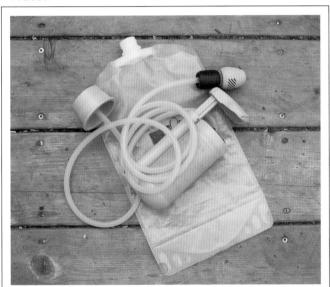

- In saltwater paddling locations, you may have to bring all your own freshwater.

- Collapsible one- to two-gallon water bladders are much easier to stow in your hatch than rigid containers.

- If you will have a freshwater source, you will still need to treat it:

- Bring water to a rolling boil for at least five minutes, dissolve iodine tablets for at least twenty minutes or, most effective, use a hand-held pump water filter/purifier.

Staples
- Condiments: ketchup and mustard packets, soy sauce, and oil in small bottles
- Spice kit
- Powdered milk, eggs
- Tea, coffee, hot cocoa, powdered drinks, bouillon cubes
- Sugar and creamer (either powdered or canned evaporated milk)
- Peanut butter and jelly
- Dried or canned soup, ramen noodles
- Oatmeal, rice, and pasta

EXPEDITION PLANNING

PACKING
Take everything you need and keep it dry

Packing a kayak for multiday trips is an art. It's well worth taking the time to think through what you need and how you will pack it ahead of time.

We learned through trial-and-error. When we started, we didn't have a lot of drybags. We put clothes in plastic grocery bags and found that they usually get holes in them and leak!

Our sleeping bag and tent have gotten wet when a hatch cover leaked. So basically anything you really don't want to get wet should be in a drybag.

The other mistake we made early on was buying large drybags that once filled were a struggle or impossible to squeeze into our hatches.

Smaller items and bags make it easier to load the kayaks to

Drybags

- Drybags come in various sizes, measured in liter capacity. For stowing in kayak hatches, you'll typically use the five- and ten-liter bags.

- They are made of heavy duty vinyl or coated nylon.

- They should have a roll-top closure that secures with buckles.

- Designate specific colors for certain items. Clear drybags allow you to see what's inside—good for food items.

Compression Sacks

Be sure to properly close sacks for a watertight seal.

- Waterproof compression stuff sacks allow you to cinch bulky soft gear like sleeping bags, tents, and clothing into more manageable sizes.

- Pack very tightly at the bottom to avoid air pockets. Stuff a sleeping bag or tent by grabbing handfuls

  and pushing firmly to the bottom.

- Cinch the drawing tight, fold the waterproof opening, and cinch down the four straps surrounding the bag.

- Label bags or have different colors for specific items.

their fullest, and believe me, on a multiday trip, you will probably need every inch of space.

If you're not ready to invest in a bunch of bags, many outfitters will rent them to you for your trip, especially if you are renting boats from them.

Well worth the investment, however, are drybags specifically made for your valuable electronics, like camera, GPS unit, and marine radio. You'll put these bags to good use on your day trips as well.

ZOOM

Tips for packing food: Put nonperishables in a clear drybag, hard items on the bottom, squooshables on top. Put all the ingredients for each meal in a large zip-top bag. Take items like granola bars and oatmeal out of boxes and put them in a zip-top bag. Freeze anything you can: soup, meat, water bottles, or juice to keep other things cold in a soft-sided cooler.

Food

- Scale down the amount of food you keep cold to one or two small soft-sided coolers that can fit into a hatch.

- Instead of taking up space with ice or cold packs, freeze food or water bottles and let them thaw along the way.

- Be sure that raw, thawing meat is in a watertight container so it doesn't contaminate other food.

- Nonperishables can go into a clear drybag. Cans, apples, or oranges can go loose in the hatch, filling up small spaces.

Keeping Valuables Dry

- Cameras, cell phones, iPods, marine radios, GPS units, and even car key fobs can be ruined with just a splash of water.

- Place these types of items in a number 5 drybag or purchase see-through bags made specifically for these items.

- You can even get voice-through, soft bags for cell phones and marine radios.

- Good waterproof digital cameras are relatively inexpensive these days.

EXPEDITION PLANNING

LOADING THE KAYAK
It's like putting together a puzzle

With canoes or large, open-cockpit tandem kayaks, you can put your gear in larger drybags and pretty much toss them in. Do keep weight centered, low and distributed evenly.

With sea kayaks, you have to give more thought to what items will go where, especially for multiday expeditions.

Smaller bags work best for two reasons: They are small enough to go into the hatch opening, and it's easier to fill the spaces inside the storage compartments with lots of smaller items rather than several large ones.

Use every bit of space wisely by breaking down large items (tent, poles, stakes) into small units and using small drybags and slipping/stuffing small items around them.

Nest your pots and pans and store smaller items like cans inside larger pots.

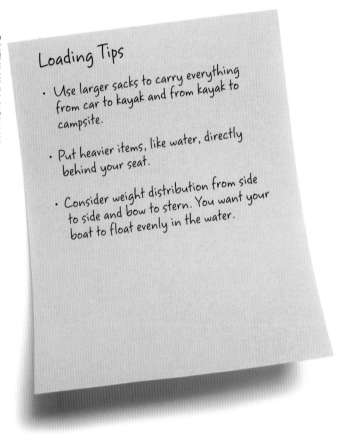

Loading Tips

- Use larger sacks to carry everything from car to kayak and from kayak to campsite.

- Put heavier items, like water, directly behind your seat.

- Consider weight distribution from side to side and bow to stern. You want your boat to float evenly in the water.

Packing the Hatch

- Place a collapsible water bladder directly behind the kayak seat.

- Next, add other heavy items like nesting pots, mess kits, loose cans of food.

- Put bulky drybags containing sleeping bag and clothes in the widest part of the hatch.

- In the far reaches of the bow and stern, place narrow items like rolled-up sleeping pads, the tent, and poles.

Waterproof compression sacks are terrific for clothes, tent, and sleeping bags.

Put heavy items closer to the kayaker's body (center of the boat) to distribute weight evenly front to back and side to side.

It's worth doing a trial run-through at home to be sure everything will fit. It's not fun to find out at the launch site that your sleeping bag or tent poles won't fit.

Day Hatch

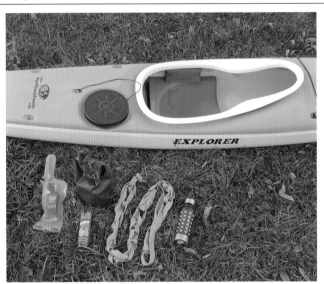

- A small day hatch directly behind your seat is extremely handy for items you want within reach.

- These items may include safety aids like a marine radio, flares, headlamp, handheld compass, and small first-aid kit.

- Also include a personal water bottle, snacks, toilet paper, knife, car keys, and cell phone.

- If you don't have a day hatch, have these safety and personal items in a small drybag in the cockpit, between your knees.

Deck Storage

Try to have only the essentials on the deck of your boat.

- Wrap your bilge pump in the paddle float and put it under a bungee within easy reach, like directly behind your seat.

- A spare paddle should be stowed under bungees on the stern deck. Hydration systems like CamelBak fit nicely under the bungees

directly behind your seat.

- A chart in a waterproof case should be under the front deck bungees.

- If there's not a recessed built-in compass, have the kind that attaches via clips and bungees.

LOW-IMPACT PADDLING
Leave the site as if you'd never been there

The motto for traveling in the outdoor world is "Leave No Trace," which is both a set of ethical practices and a nonprofit organization (www.lnt.org).

While on the water, don't throw trash, cigarette butts, or even extra bits of food into the water. Sea life simply is not accustomed to eating the way we are.

Fishing line, or monofilament, and hooks can be deadly to birds and other wildlife. Carry a knife and collect snagged monofilament. Some boat ramps have disposal tubes for recycling it.

Beaches and shorelines are environmentally sensitive areas. When landing or camping on them, be sure to follow Leave No Trace practices as well as any specific regulations of the land-owning entity.

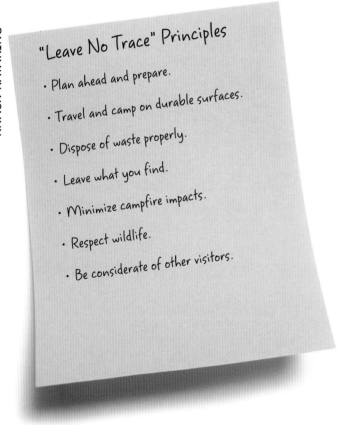

"Leave No Trace" Principles

- Plan ahead and prepare.
- Travel and camp on durable surfaces.
- Dispose of waste properly.
- Leave what you find.
- Minimize campfire impacts.
- Respect wildlife.
- Be considerate of other visitors.

Human Waste

Use a gardener's or backpacker's trowel to dig a cathole.

- Make sure everyone on the trip knows how to handle bathroom breaks in the wild.

- Urinate in the water. For solid human waste, dig a cathole 6 to 8 inches deep at least 200 feet from water, camp, and trails.

- Cover and disguise the cathole when finished. Pack out toilet paper and hygiene products in a zip-top bag.

- Some particularly sensitive areas require you to use a portable toilet, nicknamed a "boom box."

Avoid walking on dunes and fragile vegetation: Doing so contributes to erosion. Camp at least 200 feet from water and try to use established campsites. Do not alter the landscape by digging trenches or moving large stones or logs or trampling vegetation. If there is not a fire ring, don't build one.

When you break camp, do a sweep for any trash. Ideally the site should look as if you'd never been there.

Keep It Small

- If fires are not allowed, don't build one.

- Keep a fire small and burning only for the time you are using it.

- Limit the size of branches to no larger than your wrist.

Piling large logs or long limbs that extend past the fire ring is asking for trouble.

- Be aware that sparks from a large fire can fly quite far and ignite brush.

Respect Wildlife

- Observe from afar, using binoculars or a camera with a zoom lens.

- Avoid flushing birds from their perches and especially nests. Fleeing uses vital energy and leaves eggs or young vulnerable.

- Avoid unintentional feeding: Animals habituated to human trash or food can become a nuisance or even aggressive.

- Hang food and trash in a bear bag or place them in a secure hatch with straps. Flip the boat over for added security from dexterous raccoons.

WASH
Clean your boat and gear after every trip

I've always viewed washing my kayak as step 1 in boat maintenance. We paddle primarily in saltwater environments, so a good rinse-down helps prolong the life of both kayak and gear. But we use this five-minute exercise after every trip to also check deck fittings and hatch rims. We'll spray the mud or sand that's collected in the skeg box, look to the grab loops for any fraying, and give the foot pegs a squirt of corrosion

block if they don't slide easily.

No doubt the elements are hard on your gear. Skanky river water that puddles in your kayak cockpit can be a nuisance the next time you go river boating. Saltwater will corrode zippers on your PFD and wear out thin nylon spray skirt material.

Here's something else to think about: your car! When you transport sea kayaks on your roof, saltwater and sand will drip

Boat and Car

Clean Inside

Use a large, soft sponge to get sand, mud, and the last ounces of water out of the cockpit.

Boat and Car

- Hose saltwater, mud, sand, and other debris off the hull of your kayak after each trip.

- If necessary, use a large, soft sponge to wipe off dirt or debris, being careful not to rub sand and scratch the gel coat.

- A bucket of warm soapy water and a sponge may be needed for stubborn stains.

- Don't forget to hose off the roof of the car, paying attention to the roof racks and fittings.

Clean Inside

- Use a hose to spray inside the cockpit, behind and under the seat, and all around the foot pegs to loosen mud and sand.

- Flip the kayak over to empty all the water you can. It helps to have two people, one at each end to tilt one end down and then the other.

- If lifting isn't possible, rest the boat on its side, either on the ground or on sawhorses.

- Use a bilge pump to remove all the water you can.

onto the roof. We learned the hard way that if you don't hose off the roof of your car, you develop rust spots and corrosion. The water runs down into the gunnels around the windows and back hatch or trunk.

You can hose off your boat while it's still on the car or resting on the ground or on sawhorses.

We have a boat and gear washing station in our yard, which makes it easy to wash everything after each use (we paddle in saltwater).

······· **YELLOW ● LIGHT** ·······

Open hatches to be sure that they are dry and that you haven't left anything, like lunch or trash! Use a sponge to wipe out any dirt or water. If hatches are very dirty, use a hose to rinse, then a bilge pump and large sponge to empty.

Wash Gear

Hang wet gear to dry thoroughly but not in direct sunlight.

- Rinse all gear with fresh water: PFD, spray skirt, paddle, paddle float, and bilge pump.

- Have a large barrel as a dunk tank or hose gear off while it is hanging on a line or fence.

- Paddling jackets and pants can also be simply rinsed off.

- If they are heavily soiled, run them through a delicate wash cycle in your washer. Be sure to follow care instructions.

Boat Inspection

- During washing is a good time to inspect your boat. Look for:

- Deep gashes in plastic boats or scrapes in the gel coat of Kevlar and fiberglass boats

- Fraying or worn hatch cover straps

- Plastic parts that are broken or turning white

- Loose bungees and deck lines

- Corroded, loose, or missing bolts or buckles

- Worn seat cover

- Hatches that might be leaking

CARE & REPAIR

217

PROTECT & STORE BOATS
Prolong the life of your investment

Over time the sun's rays will fade the color of plastic, fiberglass gel coat, and carbon fiber. Eventually the material will degrade as well. A plastic boat left in the hot sun will literally bend and warp.

Don't store your boat in direct sunlight, especially if you live in a southern climate. Periodically use an ultraviolet protectant on your boat and paddle.

When the boat is not in use, cover your cockpit with an appropriately sized cockpit cover to keep water, dirt, insects, and animals out of it.

We have seen birds build nests in open cockpits and have had spiders crawling in them. I can't think of anything worse than being on the water and finding out there's a snake crawling around your legs!

Protectant

Just spray on a clean, dry surface and then wipe dry.

- We like 303 Aerospace Protectant, equivalent to 40 SPF sunscreen or Bow to Stern, an all-surface protectant.

- How often to apply? Always at the beginning and end of the paddling season.

- Reapply more often if water does not bead or if the color starts to fade.

- You can also apply 303 Fabric Guard to life jackets.

Cockpit Cover

- When the boat is not in use, protect your boat's cockpit from rain, insects, and dirt with a cover made of sturdy, medium-weight coated nylon.

- Look up your boat model on the cover manufacturer's size chart to get the exact fit.

- The cover should have an adjustable bungee drawstring and double-stitched seams.

- While driving, attach the tethered clip to the boat's deck bungee to prevent it from flying off while in transit.

The cover manufacturer should have a sizing chart to allow you to look up the make and model of your boat to get a cover that will fit exactly.

At the end of the paddling season, give your boat a thorough cleaning, inspection, and treatment with protectant. Store it in a clean, dry place, like a garage or shed, preferably suspending it from the ceiling with straps or resting it on padded sawhorses.

Store

Always store a boat with the cockpit cover on.

- You can store your boat on padded sawhorses placed approximately where the bulkheads are.

- Place inside a garage or shed or under a carport, as long as it is out of direct sun.

- Set the kayak on its side and lean it against a wall. Plastic boats can also be stood on end and leaned vertically against a wall.

- Always put the cockpit cover on and latch down the rudder if you have one.

Hang

- Hang your boat from the ceiling with slings made of wide nylon webbing.

- Run two slings around the hull of the boat, approximately where the bulkheads are.

- This reduces stress on the hull and also frees up floor space in your garage or shed.

- Do not use the toggle straps to suspend your boat because they will wear out over time, and plastic boats may actually bend and deform.

PROTECT & STORE GEAR
If taken care of, your gear should last many years

If you were to add up the cost of all your gear and clothing, it's probably more than you paid for your boat!

Take good care of your equipment, and it should give you years of use. Even if you're not that happy with an item, don't let it wear out so you'll have an excuse for a new one! You can always give it to someone else when you upgrade.

Life jackets, spray skirts, gloves, and paddling clothes left in a wet heap will not last very long at all. Saltwater will fade the fabric and quickly corrode the zippers and make them stick. Even if it was used only in freshwater, wet gear will smell from mildew and become unpleasant and make you very unpopular!

Find a dry place in your house and store all your paddling gear so you know where it is. A large plastic tub works well.

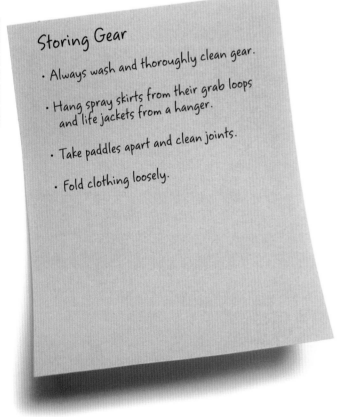

Storing Gear
- Always wash and thoroughly clean gear.
- Hang spray skirts from their grab loops and life jackets from a hanger.
- Take paddles apart and clean joints.
- Fold clothing loosely.

Paddles

- Take two-piece paddles apart. Clean and inspect the joints.

- Use a bottle brush to clean the inside.

- If the joint fit is very tight, use fine sandpaper to smooth the connection.

- Lean paddles against a wall or hang by brackets at the throat of the blade.

Or each paddler in the family can have a ventilated duffel or large mesh bag for all his or her own gear. This way, all you have to do is grab and go, knowing you'll have everything you need when you get to the water.

Spray Skirts

- Thoroughly rinse with fresh water and hang to dry.

- If the skirt is soiled or smells of mildew, you can run it through a delicate wash cycle along with your paddling clothes.

- Use neoprene wash or just plain water.

- Tears in neoprene can be repaired with a product like Aquaseal.

Life Jackets

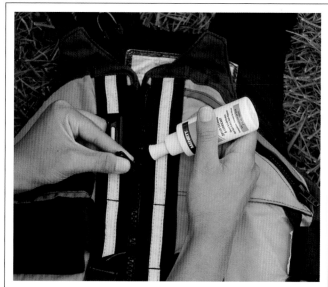

- Clean with fresh water and let dry thoroughly.

- Apply lubricant to zippers and a protectant like 303 Fabric Guard to fabric.

- Loosen straps so that the buckles aren't holding the fabric in the same place all the time.

- Place jackets loosely in a crate or tub or hang on a hanger. Avoid hanging them from one shoulder strap on a nail.

PLASTIC KAYAK REPAIR
Keep your boat afloat

Plastic kayaks only seem indestructible. The truth is that Murphy's Law applies here as much as anywhere: At some point, something will go wrong, and you'll need to make a repair.

Plastic kayaks don't age well. Sunlight softens the plastic material. Bulkheads lose their seal, rudder cables fray and break, and skeg cables may kink.

The most severe injury is a hole in the boat. Given the boat's thickness and rigidity, this would seem an unlikely scenario. Freak accidents notwithstanding, certain parts of a kayak do suffer more wear than others. One such spot is the stern keel. When you launch from shore, it is the stern keel that scrapes the concrete boat ramp or gravel shoreline. Over time, without care, it becomes soft and ultimately punctures.

A friend's boat suffered at an oyster reef. The damage was

Tools of the Trade

- Plastic weld
- Small propane or butane torch
- Putty knife
- Pliers, screwdriver, wire cutters
- Extra nuts and bolts
- Rudder or skeg cable
- Duct tape
- Wet/dry sandpaper

Cosmetic Repairs

- Dents in a kayak occur if it has been left out in direct sunlight for long periods.

- Heat and pressure are the solution to this common problem with plastic boats.

- Heat the area with a hair dryer and apply pressure to pop out the dent.

- If it is a persistent problem, use a cinder block or other heavy object to keep steady pressure on the dent.

more of a slice in the hull, not a hole, and several months of sleuthing were needed to pinpoint where this slow leak occurred.

Not all damages are as severe as a hole. Plastic kayaks left out in direct sunlight are prone to denting, and their hulls can get a washboard-like appearance.

If the repairs are cosmetic, you can heat the plastic and remold the dent or dimple. If it's a hole you're dealing with, melt lengths of plastic weld and spread them over the hole with a putty knife.

Repairs made on the go, say, in the middle of an expedition, are often temporary in nature. Duct tape has kept many a boat afloat until the paddler can make it ashore and find the right materials for a repair.

Reinforce the Keel

- The stern keel is a high-risk area for softening and possible holes in the kayak.

- Reinforce this area with plastic weld. KC Welder (www.urethanesupply.com) is a well-known, dependable product.

- You can also use G/flex by West System. This epoxy-based product adheres to plastic (not all epoxies do).

- Apply strips of fiberglass cloth soaked in G/flex along the keel as a protective strip.

Sealing Bulkheads

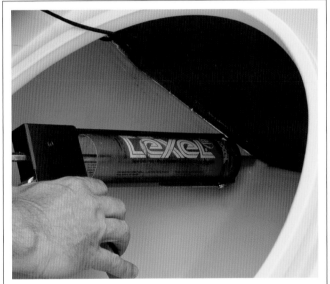

- Plastic boats flex, and as a result the seals that keep bulkheads in place may crack with age.

- A cracked bulkhead will leak water into the hatches, which ideally should remain dry and watertight.

- Your kayak manufacturer may recommend what kind of marine sealant is best for your boat.

- Make sure the marine sealant is compatible with plastic material and can get wet.

FIBERGLASS REPAIR
Gel coat and fiberglass require extra care to repair

The prospect of fixing a hole in a composite boat is often daunting enough to send kayakers out looking for a quality fiberglass repair shop.

That's one option and was the tact we took for the first few years after we bought our composite boats.

Our attitudes have changed as our boats aged. We decided that small repairs, like fixing scratches or gouges in the gel coat, were simple enough that we could save time and money by fixing them ourselves. Plus, we got back on the water quicker.

Fixing fiberglass and gel coat can be divided into two broad categories: prepare the materials and make the repair.

Make yourself familiar with such products as acetone. Women may be familiar with this as the main ingredient in

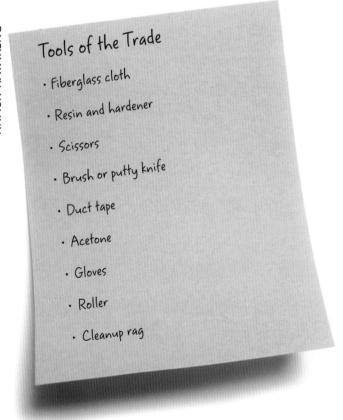

Tools of the Trade

• Fiberglass cloth

• Resin and hardener

• Scissors

• Brush or putty knife

• Duct tape

• Acetone

• Gloves

• Roller

• Cleanup rag

Minor Gouges and Scratches

• Order from your kayak manufacturer gel coat that matches your boat color.

• Prepare the surface around the gouge or scratch with sandpaper. Clean it with acetone.

• Mix the gel coat repair according to directions. Apply with an applicator.

• After the gel coat has hardened, sand it down so it is flush with the rest of the boat.

nail polish removers. It's also an effective cleanser. In boat repairs, you will use it to prepare the surface for a patch.

Fiberglass itself is material that should be handled with care. The edges of fiberglass cloth (which usually comes in rolls) fray easily. Fiberglass matte flakes easily, and its many small fibers can become itchy annoyances. Fiberglass comes in different thicknesses as well. Depending on the repair, you may want a sturdier cloth.

Resin, mixed with a hardener, is the liquid that makes fiberglass stiff and holds it in place.

When you make these repairs, be sure to work in a well-ventilated area. Wear gloves and wear a mask over your mouth and nose at all times to keep from directly inhaling the fumes from resin or gel coat. These products tend to harden quickly, so have a clear idea of the steps you will be taking and have all materials at hand to avoid delays.

Fiberglass Repairs

When you cut the fiberglass cloth, be careful that the edges do not fray.

- Prepare the surface around the hole by sanding it and wiping it down with acetone.

- Cut fiberglass cloth to cover the hole. You will use several layers for strength, each one slightly smaller than the last.

- Wet the fiberglass in a resin that has been mixed with hardener.

- Apply to the hole. Smooth with a roller. Let dry and sand the patch in preparation for another layer.

Rudder and Skeg Repairs

- A common failure with rudders and skegs is a broken or kinked cable.

- Keep the right length and size of cable on hand for quick repairs.

- Rudder repair kits supply you with the swags, nuts, and bolts that you will need to attach the cable.

- You'll need a pair of pliers, wire cutters, a screwdriver, and crimpers to make the repair.

ACCESSORY REPAIR
Prevent small repairs from becoming big problems

Apart from holes or cosmetic fixes, the types of repairs you'll face will involve the accessory or mechanical parts of the kayak.

Rudders are infamous for breaking altogether. The rope by which you deploy the rudder may break, or the entire unit may bend if the kayak is dropped.

Skegs are hardly more reliable. The skeg cable (the wire that runs from the skeg slide near the cockpit to the skeg

fin) is prone to kinking if you don't pull the skeg up upon landing on a beach. One day while Bill was exploring a tight mangrove creek in the Florida Keys, his skeg deployed accidentally when a tree branch brushed the control knob. Later he humped the kayak over a submerged log, which hit the deployed skeg, crimped the cable, and rendered it useless until he replaced the cable. Accidents do happen!

Rudder Assembly

- Rudders are controlled by cables connected to your foot pegs.

- If a cable breaks, you must replace the cable by attaching a new cable between the foot peg and rudder.

- The cable is attached with a swag, a small piece of metal that holds the cable in a loop.

- A pair of crimpers is needed to clamp the swag down on the cable and hold it in place.

Seat

- If your seat cracks or breaks, you can replace it with one shaped from closed-cell foam.

- Seat backs will also fail from time to time.

- Examine how your seat back attaches to the seat or

kayak and bring the proper nuts and bolts, plus tools, to fix it.

- In a pinch, a small drybag or a rolled foam sleeping pad makes a very serviceable back rest.

What else can go wrong? Foot peg rails can loosen, bungees can fray and break, and seat back straps may fail.

Learning what the stress points are on a kayak and where they're likely to fail is the first step toward repairing them. Look to see how your seat back strap is attached and provision yourself with the tools and materials to make a fix if necessary.

The small buckles and tri-glides that help secure a hatch cover cost mere pennies yet can mean the difference between a watertight hatch and a leaky hatch.

Above all, perform a thorough inspection of your kayak after each trip. Remember the advice about boat washing? It's the first step in boat maintenance.

Hatches

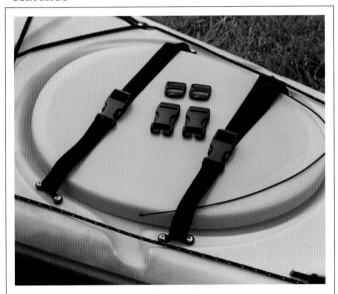

- If your hatch is secured with straps and buckles, it is a good idea to carry or have handy replacement straps and buckles.

- Tri-glides are the small slotted pieces of plastic through which straps are threaded that make it possible to tighten or loosen the straps.

- Rubber hatch covers can lose their seal or crack and split with age and too much sun exposure.

- Use 303 Aerospace Sealant to keep your rubber hatch covers pliable and reliable.

Deck Lines

- Deck lines are more than cosmetic. They become critical grab spots during a rescue.

- These lines can fray, start to break down due to sunlight exposure, or break under sudden pressure.

- Carry replacement rope with you or have it handy for a quick repair when you get off the water.

- While you're at it, double-check the deck fittings through which you thread the deck lines to be sure they're secure.

SKILLS DEVELOPMENT

Organizations

American Canoe Association (ACA), www.americancanoe.org

American Whitewater, http://americanwhitewater.org

British Canoe Union (North America), www.bcuna.com

Nantahala Outdoor Center, www.noc.com

National Outdoor Leadership School (NOLS), www.nols.edu

U.S. Coast Guard Auxiliary, www.uscgboating.org

Books

Foster, Tom, and Kel Kelly. *Catch Every Eddy . . . Surf Every Wave*. Outdoor Centre of New England, 1995.

Hanson, Jonathan. *Complete Sea Kayak Touring*. Ragged Mountain Press, 2006.

Jacobson, Cliff. *Basic Essentials Map and Compass*. Falcon, 2007.

Johnson, Shelley. *Sea Kayaking: a Woman's Guide*. Ragged Mountain Press, 1998.

Nealy, William. *Kayak the New Frontier*. Menasha Ridge Press, 2007.

Seidman, David. *The Essential Sea Kayaker*. Ragged Mountain Press, 2000.

Tilton, Buck. *Wilderness First Responder,* Second Edition. Falcon, 2004.

Walbridge, Charles, and Wayne A. Sundmacher Sr. *Whitewater Rescue Manual*. Ragged Mountain Press, 1995.

Washburne, Randel. *The Coastal Kayaker's Manual,* Third Edition. Globe Pequot Press, 1998.

DVDs

Instructional videos and DVDs can be invaluable in learning skills, particularly rolling. www.paddling.net offers many DVDs, and world renowned paddler Nigel Foster has an entire series.

Online

www.paddling.net has lots of tips and articles for paddlers.

Magazines

Canoe & Kayak, www.canoekayak.com

Kayak Fishing Magazine, www.kayakfishingmagazine.net

Paddler, http://paddlermagazine.com

Sea Kayaker Magazine, www.seakayakermag.com

Diving/fishing

www.kayakfishing.com, www.scubadiving.com, www.kayakdiving
  .com

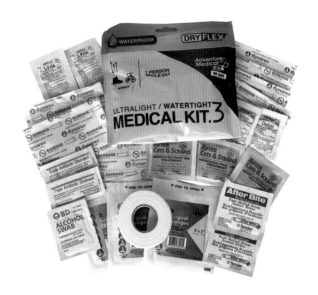

First aid/safety

Adventure Medical Kits, www.adventuremedicalkits.com

American Red Cross (CPR and first aid training), www.redcross.org

Canine First-Aid Kits, http://outdoorsafety.net

National Hurricane Center, www.nhc.noaa.gov

National Lightning Safety Institute, www.lightningsafety.com

TRIP PLANNING

Weather/tides

NOAA's National Weather Service, www.nws.noaa.gov

Tides for U.S. coastal waters, www.saltwatertides.com

Weather Underground, www.wunderground.com

Charts

NOAA's online nautical charts, www.nauticalcharts.noaa.gov

Camping

Bureau of Land Management, www.blm.gov

Burnham, Bill, and Mary Burnham. *Knack Car Camping for Everyone*. Globe Pequot Press, 2009.

Jacobson, Don. *The One Pan Gourmet*. Ragged Mountain Press, 2005.

Leave No Trace, brochures, books, and online resources, www.lnt.org

National Park Service, www.nps.gov

Pearson, Claudia. *NOLS Cookery*. Stackpole Books, 2004.

Reserve America, www.reserveamerica.com

U.S. Wildlife Refuges, www.fws.gov/refuges

White, Linda. *Cooking on a Stick*. Gibbs Smith, Publisher, 2000.

Water trails

There are many water trails throughout the United States. Some we love are the Florida Circumnavigational Saltwater Paddling Trail (http://floridapaddlingtrails.com), the Maine Island Water Trail, www.mita.org), and the Everglades Wilderness Waterw Check out http://americaswatertrails.org for a comprehensive list

Adaptive paddling

American Canoe Association Adaptive Paddling Workshops, www .americancanoe.org

Canoeing and Kayaking for Persons with Disabilities, available fro ACA, www.americancanoe.org

Equipment: http://adaptivepaddling.org, http://propelpaddles.co www.disabledadventurers.com, www.getkayaktive.com, www.kay dock.com

BUYER'S GUIDE

www.Paddling.net has an online guide to gear and kayak manufacturers grouped by type as well as classified ads for used boats.

Magazines like *Sea Kayaker, Canoe & Kayak,* and *Paddler* publish annual buyer's guides.

Major kayak manufacturers
(Specialties in parentheses)

Airis Kayaks (inflatable), http://walkerbay.com

Bic Sport North America (fishing, inflatable), www.bicsportkayaks.com

Chesapeake Light Craft (wooden boat kits), www.clcboats.com

Current Designs, http://cdkayak.com

Easy Rider Canoe and Kayak (take-apart, sailing), www.easyriderkayaks.com

Eddyline Kayaks, www.eddyline.com

Emotion Kayaks (fishing), http://emotionkayaks.com

Epic Kayaks, www.epickayaks.com

Feathercraft Products (folding), http://foldingkayak.com

Folbot (folding), www.folbot.com

Heritage (fishing), http://heritagekayaks.com

Hobie Kayaks, www.hobiecat.com

Hurricane Kayaks, http://hurricaneaquasports.com

Impex Kayaks, http://impexkayak.com

Innova Recreational Products (inflatable, whitewater), www.innovakayak.com

KayakPro, http://kayakpro.com

Klepper America (folding), http://klepperamerica.com

Malibu Kayaks (sit-on-top, fishing), http://malibukayaks.com

Native Watercraft (sit-on-top, fishing), http://nativewatercraft.com

NC Kayaks, http://nckayaks.com

Necky Kayaks, www.necky.com

Nigel Dennis Kayaks, http://seakayakinguk.com

NRS (whitewater, inflatable), www.nrsweb.com

Ocean Kayak (sit-on-top), www.oceankayak.com

Old Town Canoe Co., www.oldtowncanoe.com

P&H Sea Kayaks, http://phseakayaks.com

Pelican International (fishing), www.pelicansport.com

Perception, www.perceptionkayaks.com

Prijon Kayaks Wildwasser Sport USA Inc. (whitewater), http://wildnet.com

Pygmy Boats Inc. (wooden kits), http://pygmyboats.com

RESOURCES

Pyranha (whitewater), http://pyranha.com

QCC Kayaks, www.qcckayaks.com

Seda, http://sedakayak.com

Shakespeare Kayaks (fishing), http://shakespearekayaks.com

Swift Canoe & Kayak, http://swiftcanoe.com

Wilderness Systems, www.wildernesssystems.com

Paddles

Adventure Technology, www.atpaddle.com

Aqua-Bound, http://aquabound.com

Bending Branches, http://bendingbranches.com

Cannon Paddles, http://cannonpaddles.com

Carlisle Paddles, www.carlislepaddles.com

Epic Kayaks, www.epickayaks.com

FoxWorx Paddles, http://foxworxpaddle.com

Mitchell Paddles, http://mitchellpaddles.com

Pacific Designs, http://pacificpaddles.com

Sawyer Paddles and Oars, http://paddlesandoars.com

Swift Paddles, www.eddyline.com

Werner Paddles, http://wernerpaddles.com

Gear, PFDs, and so forth

Astral Buoyancy, www.astralbuoyancy.com

Immersion Research (paddling clothes), www.immersionresearch.co

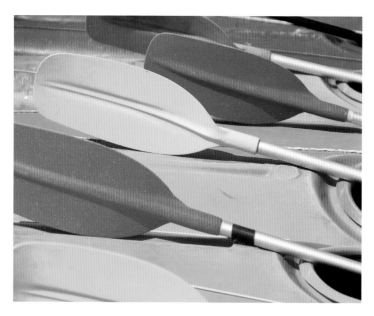

Kokatat Watersports Wear, http://kokatat.com

Lotus (PFDs), www.patagonia.com

MTI Adventurewear, http://mtiadventurewear.com

North Water Paddlesports Equipment, http://northwater.com

NRS, www.nrsweb.com

Ocean Research, www.outdoorresearch.com

Seal Line (drybags), http://cascadedesigns.com/sealline

Seals Skirts (spray skirts and cockpit covers), http://sealsskirts.com

Seattle Sports, http://seattlesportsco.com

Shred Ready (helmets), http://shredready.com

Snap Dragon (spray skirts), http://snapdragondesign.com

Stohlquist, http://stohlquist.com

Car racks
Malone, www.maloneautoracks.com

Thule, www.thuleracks.com

Yakima, www.yakima.com

Camping/clothing
Banks Fry-Bake, http://frybake.com

Base Gear.com, www.basegear.com

Camp Chef, www.campchef.com

Campmor, www.campmor.com

MSR, www.msrcorp.com

REI, www.rei.com

Sierra Designs, http://sierradesigns.com

Sierra Trading Post, www.sierratradingpost.com

SmartWool, www.smartwool.com

AUTHORS' FAVORITES
Gear we love to use

If you're reading this, it means one thing: You love gear as much as we do. Of course, all the gear in the world can't do a thing if you don't use it (say, like bringing the rain jackets when the forecast calls for rain!).

Not that there aren't other great products out there, but here are a few of our favorite things:

Kayaks
Bill: A paddling dude once described the NDK Explorer as the Toyota Camry of kayaks. If he meant it as a diss (he was, after all, repping a competitor), I've taken to liking the description: Explorers are roomy, and that means some of the creature comforts of home can come with us on multiday trips. And as with a good car, the worse the conditions, the better this boat performs.

Mary paddles Current Designs' Squamish, made of Kevlar. In key lime green, it was love at first sight. This boat weighs a scant forty-one pounds, which means she can carry it to the water herself (but don't tell Bill).

She first started paddling the plastic version and loved the handling, but the Kevlar is a much swifter animal with a little more thigh room. It has just enough storage for a multiday trip, even packing water. Speaking of which, when this light boat is empty in high winds, it benefits from some ballast in the bow, like a gear bag or a bladder of water.

Paddles
Like a first love you never quite get over, when we made the investment in carbon fiber, we started with Werner and never left.

Bill uses a Kallista carbon paddle, and Mary uses a Camano carbon with a shaft for small hands. These paddles are lightweight, two-piece for easy storage, and basically a godsend on those 15-plus-mile days.

PFDs/Spray Skirts
Mary wears a Lotus, tailored for women; Bill likes Stohlquist. Snap Dragon and Seals spray skirts round out the ensemble.

Clothing
NRS's motto is "First on the Water," and it's true. When the nas[...] weather kicks in, we don our Sea Tour Jackets with neoprene cu[...] and neck and keep on paddling.

We love SmartWool socks and long underwear for layering. They [...] not retain odor as much as synthetics. The Smart part is a blend th[...] dries quicker than traditional wool.

Footwear: Bill swears by Chacos; Mary lives in Crocs. Bill's feet st[...] warm in NRS's Desperado shoes, and its HydroSkin product is[...] wonder.

Camping
We basically transferred our backpacking gear from pack to kay[...] For about ten years, we've been using a WhisperLite stove by M[...] Marmot rain gear, and a Sierra Designs Meteor-Light tent.

When the temperatures dip, we're cozy in our Mountain Hardwe[...] Conness 30-degree down mummy bag. It compresses down to not[...] ing in OR's (Outdoor Research) waterproof compression sack.

MASTER CHECKLISTS

Essential paddling gear
- [ ] Kayak
- [ ] Paddle and paddle leash (optional)
- [ ] Life jacket/PFD (required by U.S. Coast Guard)
- [ ] Whistle and strobe light (attached to PFD)
- [ ] Helmet (required for whitewater)
- [ ] Spray skirt
- [ ] Water bottle or hydration pack
- [ ] Drybags for gear
- [ ] Towline

Navigation
- [ ] Compass
- [ ] Nautical chart
- [ ] Waterproof chart case
- [ ] Handheld compass and/or GPS unit

Safety gear
- [ ] Spare paddle
- [ ] Bilge pump
- [ ] Paddle float or block
- [ ] Headlamp and extra batteries
- [ ] Marine (VHF) radio (in a see-through drybag), extra batteries
- [ ] Strobe light, flares, dye markers, foghorn
- [ ] First-aid kit
- [ ] Whitewater: throw rope bag, rescue knife, unpin kit (carabiners, pulleys, webbing)

Personal items
- [ ] Toilet paper and small zip-top bags
- [ ] Waterproof watch
- [ ] Waterproof matches or lighter
- [ ] Multipurpose tool, duct tape
- [ ] Cell phone
- [ ] Camera (preferably waterproof)
- [ ] Binoculars
- [ ] Nose clip (for whitewater)
- [ ] Sunscreen
- [ ] Sunglasses
- [ ] Lip balm
- [ ] Bug spray
- [ ] High-energy snacks and/or lunch
- [ ] Identification guides for plants, birds, other animals
- [ ] Journal and pen

Paddling clothes
- [ ] Shoes that can get wet
- [ ] Wetsuit or drysuit
- [ ] Paddling gloves

For Warm Weather
- [ ] Wide-brimmed sun hat
- [ ] Quick-dry pants, shorts, or bathing suit
- [ ] Long-sleeved lightweight shirt for sun protection
- [ ] Spray jacket or rain jacket
- [ ] Paddling pants

For Cold Weather
- [ ] Synthetic underlayer
- [ ] Fleece midlayer
- [ ] Waterproof outer layer
- [ ] Hat and gloves
- [ ] Neoprene booties or rubber boots

Camp clothing

- [ ] Ditty bags and stuff sacks
- [ ] Shorts and pants
- [ ] Shirts
- [ ] Bathing suit
- [ ] Underwear
- [ ] Socks
- [ ] Sleepwear
- [ ] Sun hat
- [ ] Rain gear
- [ ] Hiking pants
- [ ] Hiking shoes
- [ ] Camp shoes
- [ ] Bug hood or shirt

Camping gear

- [ ] Drybags and compression sacks
- [ ] Two- or three-person domed tent(s) with poles, stakes, sand stakes if necessary
- [ ] Ground cloth
- [ ] Tarp
- [ ] Sleeping bags and roll-up pads
- [ ] Inflatable or stuffable pillows
- [ ] Single-burner stove
- [ ] Lightweight, nesting cookware
- [ ] Individual mess kits
- [ ] Clothes
- [ ] Food (see below)
- [ ] Personal water bottles
- [ ] Water bladders
- [ ] Water filter or tablets
- [ ] Light and extra batteries
- [ ] Personal toiletries
- [ ] Trowel for digging catholes, toilet paper
- [ ] Foldable, lay-flat chairs like Crazy Creek
- [ ] Small cutting board
- [ ] Large spoon, paring knife, chopping knife, spatula
- [ ] Can and bottle opener
- [ ] Matches/lighter
- [ ] Pot holder, dish towel

- [ ] Dish soap and sponge, laundry detergent
- [ ] Small trash bags (like those from the grocery store)
- [ ] Hand sanitizer

Food Staples

- [ ] Condiments: ketchup and mustard packets, soy sauce and oil in small bottles
- [ ] Spice kit
- [ ] Powdered milk, eggs
- [ ] Tea, coffee, hot cocoa, powdered drinks, bouillon cubes
- [ ] Sugar and creamer (either powdered or canned evaporated milk)
- [ ] Peanut butter and jelly
- [ ] Dried or canned soup, ramen noodles
- [ ] Oatmeal, rice, and pasta

Tools and so forth

- [ ] Mallet or hammer
- [ ] Small tool kit
- [ ] Duct tape
- [ ] Fire extinguisher
- [ ] Ropes, clothesline
- [ ] Shovel
- [ ] Multipurpose tool
- [ ] Whisk broom

Tools for Plastic Boat Repair

- [ ] Plastic weld
- [ ] Small propane or butane torch
- [ ] Putty knife
- [ ] Pliers, screwdriver, wire cutters
- [ ] Extra nuts and bolts
- [ ] Rudder or skeg cable
- [ ] Wet/dry sandpaper

Tools for Fiberglass Repair

- [ ] Fiberglass cloth
- [ ] Resin and hardener
- [ ] Scissors
- [ ] Brush or putty knife

- ☐ Duct tape
- ☐ Acetone
- ☐ Gloves
- ☐ Roller
- ☐ Cleanup rag

Pet items
- ☐ Properly sized PFD
- ☐ Bowl and bottle of water
- ☐ Food in a drybag
- ☐ Bags for waste pickup
- ☐ Pet first-aid kit
- ☐ Towel
- ☐ Proof of rabies vaccination
- ☐ Leash and collar with ID tag
- ☐ Favorite toy
- ☐ Rain jacket

Kayak fishing gear
- ☐ Rods
- ☐ Bait and/or lures
- ☐ A triangular fish bag that fits into the bow of a sit-on-top kayak
- ☐ Gear keeper clip rings to keep gear attached to your vest or boat
- ☐ Fishing gloves
- ☐ Lightweight, 1.5-pound anchor
- ☐ Sonar "fish finder"

First-aid kit
- ☐ First aid book
- ☐ Gauze
- ☐ Bandages in various sizes
- ☐ Wound dressings
- ☐ Medical tape
- ☐ Latex gloves
- ☐ Scissors
- ☐ Tweezers
- ☐ Antiseptic
- ☐ Antibiotic ointment
- ☐ Digital thermometer
- ☐ Instant hot or cold packs
- ☐ Burn ointment
- ☐ Any medications that have been prescribed by a physician
- ☐ Over-the-counter medications: ibuprofen, antihistamine, antinausea, antidiarrhea, antacid, cold medicine (children's liquid or chewable versions)
- ☐ Vitamins: multivitamin, vitamin C, and echinacea
- ☐ CPR mouth guard
- ☐ Splints
- ☐ Ace bandages
- ☐ Disposable syringe
- ☐ Emergency blanket
- ☐ Sugar packets or glucose gel for diabetics
- ☐ Sunscreen and sunburn relief
- ☐ Eye wash
- ☐ Tampons
- ☐ Snake bite kit
- ☐ Ointment relief for jellyfish or insect stings
- ☐ Motion sickness pills
- ☐ Pliers or multiuse tool
- ☐ Hypo-kit (set of warm clothing)

GLOSSARY

Aft: Toward the rear, or stern, of a boat.

Backpaddle: To paddle backward to slow down or reverse.

Bail: To empty water from a boat with a container or bilge pump.

Beam: The width of a boat at its widest point.

Bearing: The direction you want to go to reach a destination.

Bilge Pump: A hand pump used to remove water from the cockpit or hatch.

Bladder: An inflatable air bag placed inside a kayak to provide buoyancy.

Blades: The wide, flat ends of a paddle.

Bow: The front end of a boat.

Brace: A supportive stroke (see "Low brace" and "High brace").

Bulkheads: Walls inside the boat forming sealed compartments fore and aft.

Capsize: To flip over.

Carve: To hold a boat on edge during forward momentum.

CFS: Cubic feet per second, the standard measure of river volume.

Channel: A passable water route, often delineated with channel markers or buoys.

Chart: A navigational map for use on water.

Chine: Area between the bottom and the side of the boat. Hard chines are angular; soft chines are rounded.

Chute: Where a river flows between obstructions, causing a swift current.

Coaming: The lip around a kayak's cockpit onto which a spray skirt is attached.

Cockpit: Where the kayaker sits in the boat.

Deck: The top of the kayak.

Draft: The distance between the waterline and the keel.

Drybag: A waterproof bag for gear.

Drysuit: A suit designed to keep water out completely using gaskets at the openings.

Eddy: The spot in the current where water flows around an obstacle and then reverses course to fill in the space behind it.

Eddy Line: The boundary between the primary downstream current and a secondary upstream current.

Falls: A sudden drop over an edge where water falls into a pool.

Feather: To twist the shaft of the paddle so the blades set at an angle to each other.

Ferry: In whitewater, to use the current to move a boat across a current. In sea kayaking, to compensate for wind in reaching a destination.

Fiberglass: A lightweight composite boat material made by layerin resin and fabric.

Foot Brace: A pedal-like foot rest that provides greater stability and forward momentum.

Gunwale: Upper edge of the side of a boat, so named because on ships, guns were traditionally mounted here.

Hatch: Waterproof hold inside a boat to store gear, reached throug a removable hatch cover.

Heading: Direction the bow is pointing.

High Brace: A strong, supportive stroke to avert a capsize. Hands a up, elbows down.

Hole (or hydraulic): An area on a river where water backflows and can trap a boat.

Hull: The bottom side of the kayak (below the seam).

Hypothermia: Condition when body's core temperature drops to dangerous level due to cold and/or wet conditions.

International Scale of River Difficulty: Guidelines for rating the violence of a river's rapids. Categories range from Class I, marred by light ripples, to Class VI, violent whitewater that should be attempted only by advanced paddlers.

J-lean: Describes the shape of your body when edging a kayak. You achieve this position by lifting knee and hip on the side you want to raise, and pushing the hip down on the side you want to edge. Keep your torso and head on the centerline of the boat.

Kayak: A decked craft similar to a canoe and propelled by a double- or single-bladed paddle.

Keel: A strip or extrusion along the bottom of a boat to prevent side-slipping.

Kevlar: Lightweight synthetic material used in kayak construction.

Lee: An area protected from the wind.

Life Jacket (life vest or PFD): A flotation device worn by boaters to provide buoyancy in the water.

Low Brace: A supportive stroke with hands down, elbows up, and back of paddle against water.

Peel Out: To exit an eddy.

PFD (personal flotation device, life vest or jacket): Worn by paddlers for buoyancy in the water.

Port: The left side of the boat (opposite of starboard).

Portage: French word meaning to carry a boat around a rapid or obstacle.

Prusiks: A type of rope hitch used in setting up hauling systems for extracting pinned boats. Prusik cords are nylon cords of specific length and width used as tie-downs or brakes on a Z-drag.

Pry: A paddle stroke that moves a boat sideways.

Quarter: To run at an angle to the wind or waves.

Riffles: Light, shallow rapids of Class I whitewater.

Rocker: Curvature of the keel line.

Roll: To right an overturned kayak without getting out.

Rudder: A vertical blade at the rear of the kayak that steers the boat via foot pedals.

Sculling: A supporting stroke in a repeated arcing motion (like spreading peanut butter).

Shoal: A shallow area, such as a sand bar, in a body of water.

Sit-on-top Kayak: A kayak without an enclosed cockpit.

Skeg: A fin that drops down out of the hull to keep a sea kayak tracking straight.

Spray Skirt: An aid worn by paddlers to keep water out of the cockpit.

Squall: A quick-moving storm over the water.

Starboard: The right side of a boat (opposite of port).

Stern: The back end of a boat.

Strainer: A dangerous area on a river where brush or fallen trees can stop a kayak.

Strobe Light: A flashing light fitted to a life jacket to signal an emergency.

Surf: To ride a wave on ocean or whitewater rapids.

Sweep Stroke: A wide arc from fore to aft, used to turn.

Swim: To exit a boat due to capsize.

Tandem: A kayak designed for two paddlers.

Tracking: The ability of a boat to hold a straight course.

Trough: The depression between two waves.

VHF (or marine) Radio: Very high frequency radio used to call during an emergency, to communicate with other boaters, and to get current weather conditions.

Waterline: The line of water along the hull when a boat is afloat.

Wave Crest: The summit of a wave (opposite of trough).

Wet Exit: To bail out of a capsized kayak.

Wetsuit: Neoprene bodysuit that keeps you warm even when wet.

Whitewater: Turbulent, fast-moving water that flows over and around rocks, creating rapids.

PHOTO CREDITS

INDEX

INDEX